# FROM OXUS TO EUPHRATES:
# THE WORLD OF LATE ANTIQUE IRAN

# Ancient Iran Series

VOLUME 1

The titles published in this series are listed at *brill.com/ais*

**Ancient Iran Series** | Vol. I

From Oxus to Euphrates:
**The World of Late Antique Iran**

© Touraj Daryaee & Khodadad Rezakhani 2016

Touraj Daryaee & Khodadad Rezakhani are hereby identified as author of this work in accordance with Section 77 of the Copyright, Design and Patents Act 1988

Cover and Layout: Kourosh Beigpour | ISBN: 9781780835907

Printing by H&S Media © UK, 2016 | info@handsmedia.com

# FROM OXUS TO EUPHRATES:
# THE WORLD OF LATE ANTIQUE IRAN

By

Touraj Daryaee & Khodadad Rezakhani

UCI Jordan Center for Persian Studies

FARHANG FOUNDATION

2016

For Michael G. Morony,
who taught us Sasanian History

# CONTENTS

Acknowledgments ................................................................ ix
List of Illustrations ............................................................ xi
Introduction ................................................................... xiii

### Part One: Historiography of the Sasanians
A View from the Center, the Edge, and Afar

The Idea of Iranshahr in Eurasian History ........................... 7
The Idea of Late Antique Iran ............................................ 13

### Part Two: Sasanian History

Political History .................................................... 23
Sasanians and the East ......................................... 47
Ideology, Empire, and Glory ................................. 53
Economy and Trade ............................................. 57
Religion ............................................................. 63
Language and Literature ....................................... 67
Postscript ........................................................... 71

### Part Three:  Written Source

A Timeline of Late Antique Iran ......................................... 75

### Map & Genealogical Chart

    Map ...................................................................... 85
    The Sasanian Family Tree ................................. 87
Bibliography ...................................................... 91

# ACKNOWLEDGEMENTS

This book is meant to be a brief introduction to the Iranian World for those interested in history of late antiquity, and in turn, an introduction to late antique historiography for those more intimately familiar with Iranian history. Late Antiquity – a relatively recent chronological demarcation of the history of the first millennium CE – is commonly studied in the context of the Mediterranean World and in particular the empire of Rome and its continuation in Byzantium. More recently, however, many have argued for a need to consider the history of the Near East, including Iran, in the same context, giving equal attention to the political and cultural boundaries of the Sasanian Empire. We hope that this book would raise interest in a civilization that is foundational to the medieval and modern Near East and whose history is often studied merely as a footnote to Roman or Islamic histories.

We would like to thank the following people for making this publication possible. First, Mr. Milad Vandaee who made available many of the photos that he had taken in Iran. The rest were taken by Touraj Daryaee during his travels and at museums in Iran. Some of the bullae and coins belong to the Safdari collection, whose proprietor Mr. Keyvan Safdari we thank for the permission to use. Ali Razi and the Farhang Foundation, through a generous grant, made the publication of this work possible. We would like to thank Kourosh Beigpour for the cover design and for preparing the volume.

# LIST OF ILLUSTRATIONS

## CHAPTER 1

Figure. 1. Seal impression of a Sasanian official. p. xviii

Figure. 2. Coronation of Ardashir in Fars. p. 04

Figure. 3. Konar-Siyah Fire-temple. p. 05

Figure. 4. Shapur I's Triumph over the Romans at Naqsh-e Rustam. p. 10

Figure. 5. Hunting Scene: Silver Dish. p. 11

Figure. 6. Bahram II and his court at Sarab-e Bahram. p. 20

## CHAPTER 2

Figure. 7. Bust of Queen Boran. p. 21

Figure. 8. Coins of Hormizd 1 Kushanshah. p. 52

Figure. 9. Shapur II with Mithra glowing with Xwarrah at Taq-e Bustan. p. 56

Figure. 10. Seal impression of the Zoroastrian priest from Shiraz. p. 62

Figure. 11. Kerdir the Chief Zoroastrian Priest. p. 66

Figure. 12. Ostraca from Hamedan. p. 70

Figure. 13. Stucco from Seymareh. p. 72

Figure. 14. Jousting scenes at Naqsh-e Rustam. p. 73

Figure. 15. Sasanian Silver dish from the National Museum of Iran. p. 83

Figure. 16. Sasanian Empire. p. 85

# INTRODUCTION

George Rawlinson, a graduate of the University of Oxford, published *The Seventh Great Oriental Monarchy: Geography, History, and Antiquities of the Sassanian or New Persian Empire* in 1875. This was the first and only book in English on the subject of Sasanian history and remained so until Touraj Daryaee's 2008 volume, *Sasanian Iran (224-651 AD): Portrait of a Late Antique Empire*. In the meantime, there have only been a French (Christensen, 1944), a German (Schippmann, 1990) and three Russian books dedicated to the Sasanians (Lukonin, 1961 & 1969; Kolesnikov, 2012). One might wonder about the merit of paying more attention to the Sasanians and the reasons for studying them further, particularly in a new context.

The Sasanian and the Eastern Roman (Byzantine) empires were the two great late antique empires of western Eurasia. The Sasanians controlled the area between the Oxus and Euphrates rivers, which they called "*Iranshahr*" (Middle Persian *Ērānšahr*) or simply "Iran" in later literature. For both the Romans and the Sasanians, their empires were the two, and the only two, great centers of the world. All other kingdoms and civilizations were considered to be peripheries that should acknowledge the greatness of the Romans and the Persians.

The Sasanians not only organized the Oxus to Euphrates region into a single administrative and political system, but also established a defensive system that had been tried out by the

Romans earlier with the Hadrian and the Antonine walls, both built in the second century CE. The Sasanians built walls in the Caucasus, in cooperation with the Romans, and on the southern shores of the Persian Gulf. They built perhaps the longest continuous wall of antiquity, east of the Caspian Sea, which was later known as *Sadd-e Iskandar* (the Barrier of Alexander) and otherwise known as *Gizil Yilan* (the Red Snake); it was 195 kilometers long and boasted some 33 military forts (Rekavandi et. al., 2013).

The Sasanian cultural achievements are clear through the remnants of Middle Persian literature and the surviving Sasanian art. Amongst these achievements, the Sasanians are credited with staging the first polo game, specifically associated with the founder of the Sasanian dynasty, Ardashir I. The first manual in the world to discuss the game of chess as it is known today (save the invention of the queen in place of the vizier by the Spanish), as well as the game of backgammon, is in a Middle Persian text from the Sasanian period. Also, the first image of jousting as a form of sport and combat is from the third century at *Naqsh-e Rustam* in the province of Persis or Fars. These activities were among the tools needed to acquire what the Sasanians called *Frahang* or Culture in late antiquity. Furthermore, through its contacts with the Indian world, Sasanian Iran developed a literary tradition known as Wisdom Literature, beside that of the Mirror for Princes genre. The now lost Sasanian text of *Hazār Afsān* (One Thousand Tales), through its translations and adaptation into Arabic, might in fact be the basis for the collection of mediaeval Islamic tales known as the *1001 Nights*. (Beyzaie 2014)

Between the third and the seventh centuries, the Sasanians were also instrumental in Eurasian trade and exchange, including the Central Asian trade route known as the Silk Road. Middle Persian terms associated with trade clearly point to the growth and development in mercantile activities during this period. For example, the Middle Persian terms for "market" (*Bazaar*, Middle Persian *Wāzār*), "a trading party" (*Caravan*, Middle Persian *Kārwān*), and "hospices for the travelers" (*Caravanserai*, Middle Persian *Kārwān-Sarāy*) still surviving even in European languages, are all terms dating from the Sasanian period. The Sasanians held a virtual monopoly on the silk trade with the Mediterranean and established emporia all the way to China and Indonesia. The Sasanian investments in agriculture and production provided the basis for a mediaeval Green Revolution in the Middle East. Their local production of carpets (Persian carpets) was famed in China, and their monopoly of pearl from the Persian Gulf was known throughout the world. Finally, their coinage was recognized as the international trade currency in Asia even through the early Islamic period.

Culturally, one can argue that in many ways the Sasanians established the roots of the mediaeval and thus also the modern Middle East. Many of the practices, traditions, and institutions that we associate with the Islamic civilization have their origins in the Sasanian period. In terms of religious organization, it is important to note that what has been called the *Millet* system in the Ottoman Empire was the creation of the Sasanians, wherein people were organized based on religious affiliation and allowed to administer their communities autonomously. Paying a poll tax (Middle Persian *gazīdag*, hence later Arabic *jizya*) to symbolize the protection of other religious communities (namely Jews, Christians, and probably Buddhists) is based on a Sasanian universal poll-tax system. Much of Islamic institutions and practices have their origin in the Sasanian period – including the important early Islamic administrative unit of *Divan*. The Zoroastrians in the Sasanian period established foundations which were the models for the later Islamic *waqf*, pious

xv

land donations, institution and possibly the institution of the temporary marriage as well.

The coinage, administration, and institutions of the Sasanians survived the fall of the empire at the hand of Muslims and were inherited by the Islamic state system. However, since the new language of the Caliphate became Arabic, the Sasanian contributions became less visible and many of the precursors to what developed in the Umayyad, and even more so in the Abbasid Caliphate, were left unacknowledged or unknown. Thus, the study of the Sasanian Empire can help define and demonstrate the continuity and importance of the Iranian world before and after the coming of Islam and in particular in the emergence of what scholars have called the Lands of the Eastern Caliphate and eventually, the Persianate World. The study of the Sasanians is thus not only important for the history of Iran, but also for larger Middle Eastern history.

On the other hand, even in the general history of late antiquity, a proper understanding of Sasanian history serves as an important corrective to the narrative dominated by the fields dedicated to a Mediterranean focus. Whereas a Mediterranean late antiquity, despite its emphasis on change and transformation, still is focused on a narrative of decline or the changes brought about by the of the Roman system, the Sasanian sphere can show a related, but slightly different view. Many of the elements of decline in the Mediterranean in fact marked a shift to the east and the rise of Syro-Mesopotamia as a center of economic and intellectual activity in the mediaeval period. Noticing the Sasanian precedence of this rise can also help in looking at the history of the late antique Mediterranean not in terms of change and transformation brought on by decline, but rather as a case of shifting geopolitical centers, this time to mediaeval West Asia.

# Historiography of the Sasanians:
# A View from the Center, the Edge, and Afar

Figure. 1. Seal impression of a Sasanian official

Considering their importance as laid out before, one may wonder why the Sasanians have not received the attention they deserve. This is partly due to a lack of conceptual frameworks for the study of Iran as a whole, but in particular for its ancient and mediaeval periods. The concept of *Iranshahr*, "the domain of Eran/Iran," as a geographical, sociocultural, and political notion that looms large in the history of the region and specifically the Persianate world has been used only by a few people, such as S. Javad Tabatabi (in terms of political ideology [Tabatabai 1388]), and Daryaee (in terms of its specific relation to the Sasanian period [Daryaee 2002]). It has not, however, been properly considered for the study of the region as a sociocultural unit, comparable to those often set up for the Roman Mediterranean or even China, or for its lasting effects. Nonetheless, the importance of *Iranshahr*, and of the Sasanians as architects of it, was clear even in Islamic times, when in 960 CE it was suggested that "Iranshahr is from the Oxus River to the Euphrates River" (Qazvini 1332, 49).

On the other hand, even starting with Rawlinson in the nineteenth century, the Sasanians have often been seen in a negative light, as inferior to and of lesser importance than their contemporary rivals, the Romans For example in relation to Sasanian art, Rawlinson states: "The bas-reliefs of the Sassanians are extremely numerous, and though generally rude, and sometimes even grotesque, are not without a certain amount of merit" (1876, 267); or "At the worst, should it be thought that Byzantine influence appears so plainly in the later Sassanian works, that Rome rather than Persia must be credited with the buildings and sculptures..." (1876, 281). As for twentieth-century works, especially those written in the post-Soviet period, the Sasanians, to use James Russell's terminology, were considered to belong to the maligned order (Russell 1986, 123).

In Soviet, and Soviet-influenced historiography, the Sasanian state represented the feudal order in which a large peasant proletariat worked the land, while the nobility sat in their manor houses and took part in *la bon vie*. In this vision, Mazdak, the Zoroastrian priest who allegedly attempted to reform Zoroastrian law in the fifth and sixth centuries, became the first communist in history and a revolutionary in line with Lenin and Che Guevara. For this style of historiography, this top-heavy, class-based society was ripe for the coming of the Arabs and Islam as agents of radical change. But it was really more modern communist ideology than textual evidence that suggested the demise of the Sasanians at the hands of egalitarian-minded Arab Muslims. Aside from their undeniable merit as historians, scholars such as Petrushevsky and Koshelenko, through the Persian translation of their texts, fueled a lopsided view of late antique *Iranshahr* that circulated and was parroted by Iranian intellectuals in Iran and "the Greater Khurasan," or Soviet Central Asia.

Another significant impact on modern views of Sasanian history came from the Islamist camp, who attempted to justify and explain the rapid victory of the Muslims over the Sasanians in the seventh century. To do this, tactical issues, long wars, and dynastic problems were given secondary importance and concentration was placed on the "oppressive" Zoroastrian priests and the system. To quote the chief propagandist of this camp, Ali Shariati: "In Sassanian history, sometimes the second class was superior to the first class and sometimes the reverse was true. Both classes were composed of rich aristocrats and greedy people who lived in ease and luxury and ruled over the people, exploited them and kept them abased. The first class, the princes and the aristocrats, did this through coercion and the second class (the Zoroastrian priests) did so through religious legitimation. The wealth of the people was usurped by both of these two classes." (Shariati 1970, 50). in this narrative, the third class is described so: "The third class in the Sassanian era was the craftsmen, small merchants, soldiers and farmers. They were the degraded masses who were impoverished, the masses whose race was unclean as it is in India. The third class had no social rights." (Shariati 1970, 50) In this naïve and fantastic exposition of history through the prism of Islamic ideology, the inequality mentioned above in fact set the grounds for the Muslims to come to Iranshahr in order to pave the way for "equality" and "brotherhood." The masses thus opened the gates of their cities to let forebearers of monotheism into the land of fire worshippers, dualists, and oppressors. Only a rudimentary glance at the Sasanian law book, the *Mādayān ī Hazār Dādestān*, p. 8, would have made it clear that even the "third class" had important social rights, were protected, and had legal access to the court and justice, comparable to any other civilization such as Byzantium in Late Antiquity. Other theorists such as Jalal Al-e Ahmad (1357, 158) and Morteza Mottahari expressed similar ideas, calling the Sasanians corrupt and a class-based society, and the Zoroastrian priests rotten to the core (1977, 89-90), as if the rest of the late antique societies were living in a different world. Many of these neo-Islamist readings too, we should notice, were initiated by the same leftist, Soviet-influenced scholarship mentioned above, in fact.

It was these Orientalist and ideological expositions that brought to the fore the idea of the Sasanians as, to use Peter

Brown's line, the venerable dinosaurs who were seen as the dark side of the moon in late antique studies (Brown 2014). One could nonetheless posit that it is the lack of attention to the functioning of the phenomenon of *Iranshahr* and the Persianate World in the context of Islamic Middle Eastern history that has provided an unbalanced picture of the region's history in the Islamic period. Where this terra incognita of Islamic history (i.e., the Persianate World) has been brought to light, it has been largely within the context of Arabic and Arabist tradition. This is nothing new and in the twentieth century, the great historian of the Middle East and Islam, Marshall G. Hodgson, provided the reasoning behind this problem: "present-day Islamic studies still suffer from the philologism of their past. Their Arabistic bias, with the neglect of the more central Islamicate areas, is only gradually being overcome" (Hodgson 1975, 41). It is certainly time to move away from the old and disjointed paradigms and in order to do this, one needs to understand and read Sasanian history in the temporal and spatial contexts within which it stands.

Figure. 2. the investiture relief of Ardashir in Fars

# The Idea of Iranshahr in Eurasian History

Figure. 3. Konar-Siyah Fire-temple

In the third century CE, the second Sasanian monarch, Shapur I, in his trilingual inscription designated his empire as *Iranshahr*, which can be translated as the "Realm" or the "Domain" of Iranians (Huyse 1999, 22). The empire of Shapur says that his empire consisted of the following provinces and regions: Pars, Parthia, Khuzistan, Mishan, Assyria, Adiabene, Arabia, Azarbijan, Armenia, Georgia, Segan, Albania, Balasagan, and in the east, Media, Gurgan, Marv, Heart, Khurasan, Kerman, Sistan, Turan, Makran, Paradene, India, the land of the Kushans up to Peshawar and up to Kashgar, including parts of Sogdiana to the Tashkent mountains and Oman on the other side of the Persian Gulf (Huyse 1999, 22-23). Hence we can assume that there was an idea of a geographical expanse that was connected to the Sasanian rule with this specific designation.

There seems to be, however, a fluctuation of the meaning and function of the term from the beginning to the latter part of Sasanian history. The third century Zoroastrian high priest Kerdir in his inscription delineates the boundaries of *Iranshahr* as what are today's nation-states of Iran, Iraq, Afghanistan, Pakistan, and parts of the Caucasus (Gignoux 189-190), and seems to provide a religious, Zoroastrian context for the designation of *Ērān* or "Iranians." However, by the second half of the Sasanian rule, most probably with the reforms of the sixth century under Kavad and his son Khusro I, non-Zoroastrians too were seen as belonging to this realm. The most instructive example is an inscription from a Christian Iranian tomb whose engraving reads: "From the dwelling of Iranshahr, from the district of Chalagan, from the village of Khisht" (de Blois 1990, 218). By the late Sasanian period, not only were the non-Zoroastrians seen as legally part of the Iranian world (Middle Persian *zan ī šahr / mard ī šahr*, "woman/man of the Empire"), but Iranshahr had gained an imperial aspect that went beyond its political boundaries. This is best captured by the late Middle Persian geographical text *Šahrestānīhā ī Ērāšahr* (Provincial Capitals of Iranshahr; Daryaee 2002), but also by the Sasanian law book the *Mādayān ī Hazār Dādestān* (The Book of A Thousand Judgments; Perikhanian 1997).

One way to explain how the concept of Iranshahr survived is to point out that the cultural norms and values from the Sasanian realm had extended beyond its political boundaries. Thus, those people who were not ethnically, but rather culturally attuned to the "values of Iranianness" (Middle Persian *ērīh*) and who followed certain norms were then considered as part of this particular cultural sphere. What is set out in the Middle Persian texts as an Iranian acquiring of *paidea* or culture (Middle Persian *frahang* / Classical Persian *farhang*), at least for certain classes of people, included learning a set curriculum. This included studying the past in the guise of the Sasanian devotional-imperial history of *Iranshahr* or the *Khoday-nameh* (*Xwadāy-nāmag*) tradition (Shahbazi, 1990 208-225), learning certain dispositions such as being balanced and not harboring extremes (Middle Persian *paymān*) (Amouzegar 2004, 32-42), learning to write in various forms, and gaining knowledge in the house of learning (Middle Persian *frahangestān*). It also included mastery of sports such as hunting, jousting, and the Iranian sport par excellence, polo (Middle Persian *Čolwēgān*). For mental keenness, chess and backgammon were suggested (Azarnouche 2013). It is possible that the primacy of Persian as the language of culture and education had its root in this late Sasanian curriculum, allowing for its further rise in the early Islamic period and its spread to greater Iran and even as far east as the Greater Khorasan (Transoxiana and beyond).

The impact of the idea of *Iranshahr* was felt long after the fall of the Sasanians. With the weakening of the Abbasids, local kingdoms in the former areas associated with *Iranshahr* began to claim prestige by connecting themselves to the past – specifically to the Sasanians or those who were mentioned in the Sasanian national history. In Khurasan, the Tahirid dynasty of Neishabur (*Nishapur*, Sasanian *Abarshahr*) in the ninth century claimed to be connected to the great Persian hero, Rustam. The Saffarid dynasty of Sistan, ruling from Zaranj, claimed descent from Khusro II, and through him to the first Iranian king, Jamshid. The Buyids in the tenth century, coming from the Caspian region, took over the Abbasid Caliphate and Baghdad and ushered in a "Shi'ite century," relating themselves to the Sasanian king, Bahram Gur. The Samanids of Bukhara and Balkh in the tenth century promoted the Persian language and claimed descent from a Sasanian general. The Ziyarids, also from the Caspian region, claimed to be related to one of the primordial Iranian hero-kings, Kay Khusro, while the Bavandids from the same region boasted descent from another Sasanian general from the time of the Sasanian king, Khusro I. Even the Ghaznavids, who were Turkic in origin and ruled from Ghazna and Bust, claimed to have married into the family of Yazdgerd III, the last Sasanian king of kings. The Afrighids Khwarzamshahs had a legend relating them to the hero Siyavash (Bosworth 1979). Such was the power of history and the Sasanian tradition of *Iranshahr*, which outlived the Sasanians themselves and in the Islamic period spread and became a great part of the memory and tradition of the people.

Even the Qarakhanids, a Turkic dynasty in Western China ruling from Kashghar and promoting Turkic language and culture all the way to the thirteen century, claimed the Iranian antihero Afrasiyab as their progenitor (Hua 2008, 341). The importance of this fact is that no matter how different one wanted to make oneself from the Iranian world, he or she still had to play within the confines of the Sasanian tradition of the *Xwadāy-nāmag* and later the *Shahnameh* (Book of Kings), which effectively defined the narrative of the past of *Iranshahr*. So the Qarakhanids had bought into the idea of a mythical Turan, which the Iranians had created as part of their history. Everyone who lived in this region, from Western China to Mesopotamia, accepted and adapted their tradition to this history.

Figure. 4. Shapur I's Triumph over the Romans at Naqsh-e Rustam

# The Idea of Late Antique Iran

Figure. 5. Hunting Scene: Silver Dish

A colleague once mentioned that terms such as Late Antiquity come with a certain baggage, one that contains much Christianity and the Roman world within it. Thus, it was concluded, it would be futile to try to include the Iranian or the Sasanian world in that schema. We believe that once in a while such baggage should be opened and its contents rearranged to make space for new contents and ideas. Otherwise we would be wearing the same clothes or have the same antiquated ideas about antiquity and the middle ages as when the baggage was first packed.

The assessment of late antiquity as synonymous with the Christian Roman world, however, was largely held as true until the publication of Peter Brown's book, *The World of Late Antiquity* in 1971. Brown himself in fact rearranged the baggage of the idea that Alois Riegl (1899) had coined as *Spätantike*. As Frank M. Clover and Stephen Humphreys in their introductory essay about Late Antiquity have stated, it is "neither medieval, nor Roman" (1989). This idea, it seems, has yet to take hold with most historians of the period, where the Roman world maintains the center of gravity.[1]

---

1. See most recently S. Johnson, *The Oxford Handbook of Late Antiquity*, OUP, 2012, where Ethiopia and Arabia are included, presumably due to their connections to the Roman Mediterranean world, but the Sasanians and all east of the Euphrates are left out.

Sections XIII and XIV of *The World of Late Antiquity* were the most crucial parts for Iranists. Here was finally a scholar of late antiquity who was discussing the period with a much more inclusive approach, one that addressed both Rome and Iran together. Persia's (Iran's) history was brought into the framework of "Late Antiquity" (Brown 1971, 167), so that in the early 1970s the traditional boundaries of the late antique world were already broken!

In 1999 in *Interpreting Late Antiquity*, Bowersock, Brown, and Grabar stated that they decided to treat as a single whole the vast geographic space covered by the Roman and the Sasanian Empires (1999, x). This approach was given a seal of approval and more detailed attention by Michael Morony's paper titled "Should Sasanian Iran be Included in Late Antiquity?" (2008). His answer was a definitive yes. Again, as Bowersock, Brown, and Grabar stated, we are trying to "begin the 21st century with fewer artificial barriers in our minds, erected between periods and regions." (Bowersock et al.1999: x).

More recently, Teresa Bernheimer and Adam J. Silverstein, in their edited work *Late Antiquity: Eastern Perspectives* (2012), give a full account of the scholars who attempted to bring the Persianate World into the late antique framework. This basically shows that while the scholarship on late antiquity slowly acknowledges the Sasanians as an important empire – counting them even on equal footing with the Romans – its history has rarely received proper treatment. Even the important publication of Brown's *The Late Antique World*, while recognizing the centrality of the Sasanians, still gives only marginal attention to their history. Bernheimer and Silverstein's *Late Antiquity* even lacks an article by a scholar of Sasanian history, and gives more attention both in the choice of editors and of authors to (early) Islamic history than to the Sasanian one that spanned the length of late antiquity.

Similarly, in a recent introductory essay Pourshariati has touched upon the importance of including the Iranian world in the framework of late antiquity, but with some caution and without considering a longer time period (Pourshariati 2013: 7). She cites her efforts in 2008 to promote the idea of late antique Iran at the Middle East Studies Association, a venue where traditionally the seventh century CE is the earliest period of interest. Pourshariati's panels at this venue under the rubric of "Recent Trends in Late Antique Iranian Studies" (Pourshariati 2013: 7) indeed energized scholars from Islamic, Jewish, and Middle Iranian Studies to come together and deal with the world of late antiquity.

However, we should note that Pourshariati's assertion that the inclusion of Iran in the field of late antiquity was uncommon prior to her efforts needs some corrective. One can begin with the earliest reference to *Finanzgeschichte der Spätantike* by Altheim and Stiehl (1957), which treats Sasanian Iran, Rome, and the Kushans under the rubric of late antiquity. Since the 1980s, Michael Morony has produced a number of studies on the economic and social history of the late antique Near East, including a two-volume edited series on the economic history of the period. One can use such examples as his "Land Use and Settlement Patterns in Late Sasanian and Early Islamic Iraq" (1994), and his study of Sasanian and early Islamic Iraq (1984). Morony's other publications, including "Economic Boundaries? Late Antiquity and Early Islam" (2004), "Landholding in Seventh-Century Iraq: Late Sasanian and Early Islamic Patterns" (1981), and many similar works were also written under the general framework of late antiquity and its context in the Iranshahr. Since the 1990s, in fact, a number of his students have become historians of the late antique Sasanian world, focusing on the economy. Cynthia Villagomez in 1998 discussed the economic history of the late antique period based on Syriac sources. Daryaee has already published a number of works on the Persian Gulf trade in late antiquity (2003, 1-16 : 2009, 57-70) and on bazaars, merchants, and trade in late antique Iran (Daryaee 2010: 401-409). Subsequent students of Morony, including Scott McDonough and Rezakhani produced dissertations concerned with late antiquity and the Sasanian Empire. The concern of Morony's student have also continued to be on the same geographical area and the same methodological and historical approach, including publications by Daryaee and others on various late antique Sasanian themes. What might have also been overlooked is the existence of *Sasanika: Late Antique Iran Project* (www.sasanika.com), which has been active since 2004 and has included a number of research papers, archaeological reports, primary sources, images, and graduate student papers. It was, in fact, *Sasanika* that commissioned the publication of Morony's now famous paper on the inclusion of Iran in the context of late antiquity in 2008. Both authors of the present volume, being among the students of Michael Morony, have thus benefited from the deep interest of their mentor on their doctoral work and their work ever since. While, due to Morony's primary interest in Arabic and Early Islamic studies, the focus on the late antique period and non-Arabic (Middle Persian, Bactrian, Syriac, and Armenian) sources was initially deemed problematic, with time this was overcome. With the aid and guidance of Claudia Rapp, eminent Byzantinist and a committed scholar of late antiquity, as well as linguistic guidance of H-P Schmidt (for Daryaee) and Martin Schwartz and M. Rahim Shayegan (for Rezakhani), the authors managed to bridge the seemingly unfordable gap of pre-Islamic and Islamic periods and bringing the late antique and early Islamic interests of their mentors together. Additional training in numismatics, archaeology, and art history has also provided the necessary tools and means of undertaking research – which seems too daunting at times.

All this varied and interdisciplinary education and study made us ready to see the Sasanians within a larger framework and as part of a series of connected-histories (to borrow from Subrahmanyam). We understood that Sasanian history is recognized as important and crucial for our Roman and Islamic historian colleagues, but that it is constantly studied from the "edges," based on the available sources. Islamic historians like al-Tabari present us with a view of Sasanian history from a temporal edge, after its fall and when it is already ripe for being analyzed and compartmentalized. Roman historians such as Ammianus Marcellinus present a limited view from a geographical edge, that of the Roman Empire. We thus use the methodological tools presented to us by our background, as well as technical knowledge of languages such as Middle Persian and Syriac, to present a possibly more regional, but fully connected, view. In this sense, our use of Middle Persian literature, which is negligible compared with Greek, Latin, or Arabic sources, is not to discern "facts" from it, but rather to understand and present a history of Sasanian *mentalité*.

Of course, there is no argument with the current trends in the study of late antiquity, as it is relatively young still. We understand that the study of late antiquity has been so far dominated by the issue of the Christianization of the Roman Empire and its transformation to the world of mediaeval Europe. In this sense, the study of Islam provides a natural parallel, allowing for a convincing comparison of Christian mediaeval Europe and Byzantium with their peers in the Umayyad and Abbasid Caliphates. The Sasanians, in this schema, are not considered as important since their religious legacy did not continue as effectively as the Christian and Muslim traditions have, rendering them essentially irrelevant to this framework. Furthermore, their absence from the Mediterranean basin made them even less important for the history of Europe, which after all is the focus of most studies of late antique and mediaeval history. Here, however, we are positing that although Zoroastrianism, the religion of the Sasanian state, might not have survived – albeit in small pockets – the end of late antiquity, the Sasanian institutions, many of which were indeed created under the dominance of Zoroastrianism, did in fact survive. These in turn morphed into familiar institutions that determined the culture of the mediaeval Middle East, in both Islamic and Christian religious settings. These institutions, ranging from warring methods to the structure of the state, influenced the mediaeval world as much as Christian Roman or the Islamic systems did, and thus present the Sasanians as a necessary part of the study of the late antique world.

Furthermore, the fluidity of the boundaries of the framework of late antiquity allow for the exchange of ideas and birth of new ideas. These range from Clover and Humphrey's concept of Late Antiquity as the period from Alexander to the Crusades, considering the study of cities and local cultures (1989, 4), to the traditional French view of *Antiquité tardive* from the third century CE and Diocletian to the fifth century CE with the fall of Rome, as demonstrated by Bertrand Lançon. We would be in favor of expanding this synchrony to Maharaja Sri-Gupta's Gupta India (320-550 CE) with its Hindu culture, perhaps to Harshavardhana's Harrsha kingdom in the seventh century. Of course the Kushans and their east Iranian successors are the other ignored traditions that are studied in isolation and without consideration of greater world history. We could pose the idea that a Eurasian late antique history, within the methodologies of global or world history, might indeed be possible, finding greater trends in the history of areas that were connected in geographical and many other senses. While this might yet be considered an idealistic fantasy, we can take comfort in the fact that pushing boundaries has always had its merits. If such suggestions seem at present unattainable or even ahistorical within the current criteria set for historical research, we must stop and consider that we might be creating our lines of comparison and connection too tightly, and, even more so, that we might be concentrating on tautological understanding of the sources and evidence that lead to preconceived notions and dead ends. One has only to look at Matthew Canepa's recent book, *Two Eyes of the Earth*, to see what can be achieved by crossing the artificial boundaries and taking up alternative sources and methodologies (Canepa 2010). This traversing of boundaries is done by quite a few scholars already, both in the temporal and spatial senses. Joel Walker, Mathew Canepa, and Tom Sizgorich are travelers who easily move across the Eurasian landscape, while Michael Morony and Parvaneh Pourshariati cross temporal boundaries to demonstrate the importance of Sasanian history for the study of the Islamic one.

We should discuss how we can or how much we have done to make the Iranian Plateau part of the Late Antique world. Some of the issues that need attention are as follows: I. Problems in periodizing Sasanian history (see Shayegan 2003); II. Iran during "Late Antiquity" vs. "Sasanian dynastic" history: Is it possible to escape the dynastic framework?; III. Regionalism vs. imperial history of Late Antique Iran; IV. Existing problems in studying Sasanian history; V. The transition period from Sasanian to Islamic Iran; and VI. What are the new ways of approaching Late Antique Iran?

Within the context laid out above, and using the methodologies described, the following pages will provide an outline of Sasanian history. We have tried to provide a useful guide to those who want to have a grasp of the basics of Sasanian history, incorporating the latest revisions that the scholarship in the field has provided. Discussions of specific issues within Sasanian history, the study of the aforementioned *mentalité,* as well as institutions and concepts are each presented in different sections, hopefully rendering the presentation accessible to both the general and the more specialized audiences who might not be intimately familiar with the period. The ultimate goal is to describe the context of late antiquity for the study of Sasanian history, and at the same time to serve as a quick guide to this lesser known of late antique entities.

Figure. 6. Bahram II and his court at Sarab-e Bahram

# Sasanian History

Figure. 7. Bust of Queen Boran

# Political History

As much as Sasanians were the progenitors of late antiquity in central and west Asia, their own roots laid squarely in the period commonly labeled "the Hellenistic Period" (Strootman 2014). The founder of the Sasanian dynasty, Ardashir ī Pabagan, was a member of a noble family of Persis, one of the so-called Hellenistic Kingdoms of southern Iran. The kings of Persis had, throughout the Arsacid rule in Iran (211 BCE – 223 CE), enjoyed a high level of local autonomy, including the right to issue coins in their own names.[2] Although the later Islamic sources present a garbled version of Ardashir's rise to power, numismatic evidence provides us with the ability to establish somewhat of a narrative. Al-Tabari, the famed Muslim historian, tells us that Ardashir's father, Pabag, was a nobleman of the court of Gozihr, the local ruler of Persis, whose daughter had already married Pabag. Ardashir himself was left in the foster care of an Argbed (fortress master) who governed the city of Darabgird, where he later took over and set up base in a rebellion against both Gozihr and later, Ardawan (Artabanus

---

2. For a general sketch of the history of Hellenistic Persis, see Josef Wiesehöfer. *Die „dunklen Jahrhunderte' der Persis: Untersuchungen zu Geschichte und Kultur von Fārs in frühhellenistischer Zeit (330- 140 v. Chr.)*. CH Beck, 1994. For coins, see most recently D. O. A. Klose and W. Müseler, *Statthalter, Rebellen, Könige: Die Münzen aus Persepolis von Alexander dem Großen zu den Sasaniden*, Munich: Staatlishe Sammlung, 2008.

IV/V), the Arsacid Great King (Daryaee, 2009, 3-5). Based on al-Tabari's narrative, Pabag was the son of Sasan, a priest of the temple of the goddess Anahid in the city of Istakhr, the capital of the province of Persis/Fars (Tabari/Bosworth, 4).

While the narrative in al-Tabari seems to be giving the entire agency to Ardashir, from the coins in fact tell us that Pabag himself had been the initiator of the rebellion, as is evident by the coins he had issued with his eldest son, Shapur. Even al-Tabari's narrative cannot quite hide this, providing the tale of a suspicious meeting between Ardashir and his elder brother prior to which Shapur dies in mysterious circumstances (Tabari/Bosworth, 8). The emergence of this new power naturally alarmed the Arsacids, but they were unable to stop the Sasanian advancements. Ardawan IV, and eventually his rival and temporary successor Vologasses/Walakhsh VI (d. 229 CE), soon fell victim to Ardashir. Ardashir thus must have been in charge of a large portion of Arsacid territories by about 224 CE, when he crowned himself King of Kings in Ctesiphon, essentially adopting the Arsacid title. Conquests in the east, particularly the takeover of the important town of Marv in northeastern Khorasan, as well as the subjugation of the territory of the Indo-Parthians in Sistan, were the final achievement of Ardashir I.

Here, we must consider the rise of the Sasanians within the context of their contemporary world. The few decades immediately preceding the rise of Ardashir were marked by unrest all around Central and West Asia and the Mediterranean. The great Kushan power in the east was already in decline, having passed its glory days of Kanishka, Huvishka, and Vesudeva. Further south of the Kushans, the Indo-Parthian kingdom, in charge of Sistan, Arachosia, and parts of Gandhara, was also in serious decline. The last Indo-Parthian king, Farn-Sasan, whose coins have survived, seems to have controlled only a fraction of the empire of Gondophares, and fell victim to Ardashir's forces. In the west and in Rome, the dynasty of the "Philosopher Kings" of Hadrian and Marcus Aurelius had descended into the militarism of the Septimians, and was on its way to the "Crisis of the Third Century." More than that, the great Arsacid Dynasty, in charge of most of West Asia since the second century BCE, had now been reduced to infighting among various claimants to the throne. Artabanus in fact appears to only have been in charge of parts of the empire, and his brother Walkhash/Vologases VI put up a resistance against Ardashir as late as 226 CE. In a sense, the organization of the Sasanian Empire appears to have been an earlier attempt at remedying the messy state of affairs in the terminal Hellenistic period and the emergence of the late antique one – something that in the Mediterranean was only achieved by the efforts of Diocletian at the end of the third century. However, it would be too simplistic to claim that these early Sasanian efforts at conquest in any way would have amounted to a conscious effort at creating a centralized state, a defining feature of later Sasanian imperial policies.

The world into which the Sasanians stepped can be characterized as one that was in a crisis of identity, and it was attempting to create new identities. Regional identities, associated with limited sociopolitical ideologies, were on the brink of being augmented, and eventually overwhelmed, by those taken from abstract notions such as religion, ideological connections, and institutions. Within this framework, the foundation of the Sasanian monarchy and its relation to its own physical reality, as well as to its ideological existence, are important avenues through which we can understand Sasanian history. (Payne 2014: 288-290)

We should consider that the rise of Ardashir himself has been understood within an essentially Roman narrative of historians such as Herodian who depict his success as a rebirth of the "Persian" (i.e., Achaemenid) Empire (Rubin, 1980). Whether Ardashir and the early Sasanians in fact were aware of the existence of the Achaemenids is a matter of passionate debate among scholars (Yarshater 1971; Daryaee 1999; Daryaee 2005; Wiesehofer 1994; Huyse 2002; Canepa 2010; Callieri 2011; Gariboldi 2006). But it is worth noting that there is enough evidence, whether later legendary narratives of the early Islamic historians or contemporary numismatic evidence, to suggest that Ardashir and his immediate successors paid at least as much attention to the eastern half of their empire as the western one. This geographical divide, in fact an administrative rationalism that was a relic of the Hellenistic period, can be used to define the Sasanians for at least the first century and a half of their existence. Sasanian activities in eastern Iran opened the door for cultural influences of the Kushans, itself a well-balanced mix of Iranian, Indian, and nomadic cultures, creating a cultural milieu that was to be influential in the formation of the Iranian identity in the later period of Sasanian history. The evidence for this regional administration and its development, as well as the cultural setting of it, are found during the reign of Ardashir's son and successor, Shapur I.

After some clashes with the Roman Empire in Syria – eventually the cause of much conflict between the two empires – Ardashir appointed his son Shapur I (r. 240-70 CE) as co-regent and retired to his home province. During the reign of Shapur I, Sasanian conquests continued in both the east and the west. There also was a significant increase in the size of the administrative apparatus, evidence used to argue for a conscious move toward imperial centralization, which was not really achieved for many centuries. At this time Armenia became a major point of contention between the Sasanians and the Romans, and it remained so until it was partitioned between the two empires in the fifth century CE (Traina 2009). Shapur famously defeated Gordianus III in 244 and forced his successor, Philip the Arab, into a humiliating treaty. The most significant achievement of Shapur against Rome, however, appears to have been his capture of Emperor Valerian, a set of events reflected in both his inscription at *Ka'aba-i Zardosht* in Fars (Huyse, 1999), as well as in a major relief located in the same vicinity. This marked a return of the Iranian military power to take control of Mesopotamia after a relatively long slump in the second and early third centuries that had allowed Roman incursions into the Near East and Mesopotamia in the terminal Arsacid period (Gyselen, 2010). Sasanian successes at this point were the cause of regional unrest and disability in Roman Syria and Egypt, best exemplified in the short but effective "Empire of Palmyra" of Queen Zenobia (Millar 1995). In only a few decades of existence, the Sasanians had managed to not only take charge of their own realm, but also to change and influence the politics of their larger region.

Several Sasanian artistic and cultural productions of the reigns of Ardashir and Shapur are worth discussing here. The famous relief of Darabgird (Levit-Tawil, 1992), whether depicting Shapur or his father Ardashir, is a clear and significant indication of how the Sasanian founders saw themselves in their world. The general scene, dismissible as a work of propaganda similar to Shapur's *Naqsh-e Rostam* relief (Hermann and Curtis, 2002), is, however, indicative of how the Sasanian king wished to be depicted. The Romans presented in the scene, as accurately as possible, are there in order to show not only the victory of the Sasanian King of Kings over the Roman Augustus, but also to demonstrate the presence of the Sasanian power itself within the political world of the time. In his inscription on *Ka'abe i Zardušt* (ŠKZ), Shapur is not simply boasting of a victory over the Roman forces, but is also announcing the reality of the existence of power within a new world, one that up to this point was understood as one of the Classical Roman Empire and the Hellenistic Arsacid Empire. In the world of the third century, where Rome was undergoing a "crisis" and change that allows it to emerge as the Christian empire of Constantine, the Sasanians were agents of change in their own world, emerging similarly as a new force in the late antique world.

Two other things are also noteworthy from the ŠKZ inscription, the first being the use of language. This is the only Sasanian inscription that is inscribed in three languages: Greek – the iconic language of Hellenism and at this point more of relic than a reality,[3] Parthian – the ethnic and presumably administrative language of the defunct Arsacids, and Middle Persian – the language of the incipient Sasanian dynasty (Huyse 2009). We could see here that Greek, as the effective administrative language of the eastern half of the Roman Empire, in fact fits the purpose of the inscription, containing the tale of Shapur's victories over Roman forces. Parthian was arguably still the prestige language of the empire, since barely three decades had passed since the fall of the Arsacids. Middle Persian, however, is a significant addition, a language that obviously will come to dominate the administration of the Sasanians and become a cultural marker of their civilization. In a way, the languages of the ŠKZ are reflective of the changing world in which the Sasanians exist, and anticipate the world that they come to fashion. A second interesting point is the tone and composition of the ŠKZ. While clearly a propaganda piece, the inscription is not an isolated creation. Similarities

---

3. In fact, in the "Hellenistic" Kingdom of Persis, where ŠKZ is located, Greek was never used as a monumental script nor as the language of coin inscriptions, unlike in other Hellenistic kingdoms like Elymais, Characene, or even the Arsacid Empire itself. On the script of Persis coins, see (Rezakhani 2016)

between it and the great Behistun inscription of Darius the Great have been known and considered by scholars (Huyse 1999; Shayegan 2011; Shayegan 2012); in a more contemporary setting, the inscription harkens back to the Rabatak inscription of Kanishka the Great (Cribb and Sims-Williams 1996; Sims Williams 2004/2008). Like the great Kushan King of Kings, Shapur is describing the boundaries of his empire, boasting of the new cities that have come under his rule, and offering religious rites in exchange for divine protection. The ŠKZ, in many senses, is evidence of the involvement of the Sasanians with the eastern and western halves of their empire, perhaps not accidentally placed at its center.

Hormizd I (r. 270-1), or Hormizd-Ardashir, was mentioned as "King of Armenia" in his father's ŠKZ inscription (ŠKZ 18). His short reign most likely left little impact on the Sasanian Empire, although he is mentioned as a good king by the later sources. His brother, Wahram I (r. 271-4) also ruled for a short period and is known primarily, like Hormizd, through his coins as well as being mentioned in the inscriptions of his father and also that of his son's chief priest, Kerdir (See below).

Wahram I's eldest son, Wahram II (r. 274-93 CE) has left several pieces of evidence of his rule, mainly in Persis and including reliefs in Bishapur, as well as being mentioned in the inscription of his high priest, Kerdir. Wahram's period appears to be one of stability and increasing introspection for the Sasanian administration. Kerdir's inscriptions seem to suggest a successful establishment of Zoroastrian church administration as the official religion of Sasanian Iran. He talks about the persecution of Manichaeans, Christians, and followers of other religions, and his own appointment as the chief priest of the country. Despite these claims, we should understand Kerdir's claims as largely a boast, as we know that during the reign of Shapur, Hormizd, and Wahram I, Manichaeism was freely promoted by its prophet Mani – until his execution by Wahram I – and that Christianity, Judaism, and Buddhism continued to be practiced in the Sasanian realm for the rest of its history. Wahram famously summoned and executed the prophet Mani "(on whom see the section on *Religion* below) and gave much power to Kerdir, a Zoroastrian cleric who had slowly gained power throughout the rules of Shapur I and his immediate successors.

Wahram's reign was all in all relatively peaceful. The weakness of the Roman Empire meant a calm western frontier, while the increasing Sasanian influence in the east at the expense of the Kushans also secured the eastern frontiers. Internal conflicts, however, presented themselves in the form of a rebellion of Wahram's brother, Hormizd (Daryaee, 2008, 34-35). The execution of Mani and the victory of Kerdir presents a fascinating case in the course of what was to become the ideological foundations of the Sasanians (Russell 1990). Mani, a native of Babylon and despite all details of his biography essentially a religious figure of Syro-Mesopotamia, presents an interesting study in the world of late antiquity within a Sasanian context. Mani appeared during the reign of Shapur I (ca. 240) and lasted until the reign of Wahram I (ca. 271). Mani's religious world was set within a Syro-Mesopotamian background, complete with a strong Christian and gnostic overtone. Indeed, Mani himself was raised in a gnostic, probably Elchasite, community, and his religion was undoubtedly one of the most successful gnostic movements in history. Mani was also a representative of the Arsacid world, one that was struggling against the changing world of the Sasanians, and in a sense was trying to set his world, which had fallen apart, into a new order (Stroumsa and Stroumsa 1988). His efforts in creating a hybrid religion, a universal religion that would help in creating a new identity, one that went beyond regionalism and even empires, was a quintessentially late antique effort, one that was initially supported by Shapur, Hormizd, and even Wahram I (Fowden 1993). On the other hand, his own figure as the "prophet" of a new religion, one who boldly declares his desire to write his own teachings, is also another glaring characteristic of late antiquity, that of the figure of a holy-man (Brown 1971). The victory of Kerdir, and the rise of Zoroastrianism, although a defeat for Mani and Manichaeism, is simply the reflection of a more successful attempt at achieving the same end, what we might be able to call the start of another ideology that sought to create identities, and in the Sasanian case, came to define the sociocultural world of the Iranshahr deeply enough for it to survive far beyond the demise of the Sasanians.

Wahram III (293), referred to in Narseh's *Paikuli Inscription* as the *King of the Sakas*, was installed on the throne through a conspiracy in the imperial administration, headed by an official named Wahnam. We have no coins of this king, and his short reign was marred in conflicts with Narseh, the third son of Shapur I. He has been called a son of Wahram II by later, Islamic sources, but there is no evidence for such identification in fact (Rezakhani 2015). Narseh, at the time functioning as the king of Armenia, managed to lead a rebellion that deposed Wahram III, a major operation that has been detailed in his inscription of Paikuli (Humbach/Skjaervo, 1978, pt. 1). The Paikuli inscription, unlike that of Narseh's father in Naqsh-e Rostam (ŠKZ), does not use Greek, but still uses Parthian as the language of its declaration. As the last reflection of the use of Parthian in the Sasanian period, it is a monument to the gradual waning of the old, Hellenistic "order" and the emergence of a Sasanian, late antique world.

The rule of Narseh (293-302 CE) coincided with the popularization and eventual adoption of Christianity in Armenia (Kettenhofen 1995), and bitter wars over that kingdom with the Roman Empire. A defeat at the hands of the Roman general Galerius resulted in the Treaty of Nisibis in 298, which allowed Tiridates III back on the Armenian throne and brought Iberia (the historical kingdom of Georgia) to the Roman sphere of influence (Daryaee 2009, 13). Around the same time, a Sasanian cadet branch was establishing a semi-independent rule in the Kushan territories, designating themselves Kushanshahs and striking gold coins in Kushan style. We are not clear about the relationship between the Kushanshahs and the main Sasanian dynasty, but presumably a certain kind of suzerainty was maintained from Ctesiphon. Kushanshahs, however, appear in Narseh's inscription as independent kings, almost equal to the Romans, and might indicate the continued importance of eastern Iran in the affairs of the Sasanians. Mention of Wahram (III) as the "King of the Sakas" as well as of the Kushanshahs and of what appear to be the autonomous rulers of various territories also indicates the lingering administrative structure of the early Sasanian period, and in fact justifies the literal use of the title of King of Kings. The title, clearly a borrowing from the Arsacids and the Kushans and eventually the Achaemenids, at least in principle shows a hierarchy of kingship, establishing the Sasanian king of kings as the *princeps* over a series of other kings. The survival of the title, even after the re-organization of the Sasanian domains and the disappearance of such a system, is another aspect of the changing world of late antique Iran.

Narseh's death in 302 brought his son, Hormizd II on the throne (Daryaee 2008, 43-44). The new king also mainly presided over the conflict with Rome on the issue of Armenia, whose king, Tiridates/Trdat III, reputedly converted to Christianity in 301 (Agathangełos/Thomson, 243-244). Hormizd was initially succeeded by a son called Adur-Narseh, who ruled only for a short while in 309 (Taffazoli, Ādur Narseh, *EIr*). There are, however, no references to him in the numismatic evidence or in the later Islamic sources, while Byzantine sources only mention his existence as the elder son of Hormizd II.

The circumstances of the birth and reign of Shapur II (r. 309-379), the longest reigning Sasanian monarch, are quite legendary and include him being crowned while still in his mother's womb and forty days after the death of his father, Hormizd II *(Mojmal ol-Tavarikh*, 34). When he came of age, he set about curbing the Arab incursions in the south and punishing the perpetrators (Tabari/Bosworth, 50-56), thus becoming known with the epithet the "Lord of Shoulders" (Arabic *Dhu-l-Aktaf*). In the east, Shapur II was faced with a major invasion by possibly the Huns who are called Chionites in the Byzantine sources (Cereti 2010) and who only agreed to form an alliance after fierce battles. This resulted in the termination of the rule of the Sasanian cadet branch, known as the Kushano-Sasanians (Dani & Litvinsky, 1996), over Bactria, and the establishment of an autonomous "Hunnic" (possibly Kidarite) rule in Transoxiana and Bactria (Amm. Marc., 17.5.1; Nikitin 1999). In the west, Shapur had to face the Romans under Julian the Apostate in 363, although that campaign was soon abandoned following the assassination of Julian by his own troops. The resulting peace treaty with Jovian put the important border town of Nisibis under Sasanian control and created a long lasting point of contention between the two empires (Blockley 1988). The long and relatively calm rule of Shapur helped bring stability to the Sasanian Empire, and established Sasanian control over both the eastern provinces and the Persian Gulf region.

If the reign of Constantine is seen as the beginning of a new, Christian Roman Empire and the proper "beginning" of Mediterranean late antiquity, the same thing can be said for that of Shapur II in the Sasanian realm, although with uncertain religious consequences. Shapur's military successes put the

Sasanian dynasty firmly in control of their realm, and the reorganization initiated by the Hunnic wars appears to have ended the system of vassal kingdoms, which had been inherited from the Arsacids. The Sasanian king of kings was now almost directly in charge of his realm and guaranteed its security without the intermediary of local autonomous powers. If the Sasanian ideal of centralization ever had a proper beginning, the reign of Shapur would appear to be a good candidate. Here, the image of the King of Kings as the princeps over other kings starts to be replaced by the image of a central ruler, subsequently to be marked as a *Kay* (Daryaee, 1995) even on his coins, and increasingly recognized ideologically as the founder of an ancient order, one that is defined progressively through the religious medium of an emerging Mazdean/Zoroastrian religious structure (Rezakhani 2014).

Ardashir II (r. 379-83 CE) succeeded his brother Shapur II, probably the result of an agreement with the latter. The relief at *Taq-i Bostan* (Tanabe, 1985; Kaim, 2009) shows an exchange of a diadem between the brothers, possibly a reward for Ardashir's bravery in the wars against Rome (Shahbazi, "Ardašīr II," *EIr).* Al-Tabari associated Ardashir II with a great purge in the Sasanian nobility aimed at curbing their increasing power, an act that resulted in his removal from the throne (Tabari/Boswoth, 67-68). The agreement between Shapur II and Ardashir II, commemorated at Taq-i Bostan, probably guaranteed the succession of Shapur III (383-388), the son of Shapur II. The reign of Shapur III is the start of a temporary weakening in the Sasanian royal power, as reported by the chroniclers. As with Ardashir II, the courtiers of Shapur III were successful in removing him, this time through causing his death under the collapsing weight of his own tent (Tabari/Bosworth, 68; al-Yaghubi, I/183). Wahram IV (r. 388-399), another son of Shapur II, seems to have had a similarly short reign. His most significant action was to be the placement of his brother *Wahrām-Shapur* (Arm. *Vramšāpuh*) on the Armenian throne. Like his brother (or perhaps father?) Shapur III, Wahram IV also fell victim to the conspiracy of the court nobles and was removed in favor of his son (or perhaps brother?), Yazdgerd I (Klima, 1988).

Although we have no indication of military involvement in any of these cases of royal coups – the conspirators are simply called the nobles – the quick succession and involuntary removal of kings seems quite similar to the Roman case in the third century and the rise of the Praetorian Guard as a "king-making" force. Whether these noble coups were backed by the military or not is not mentioned in the sources, but it would be safe to assume that the heightened militarization during the reign of Shapur II engendered a stronger military class who found an avenue for their political ambitions during the reign of the successors of Shapur.

The reign of Yazdgerd I (399-420) was the beginning of restoration in Sasanian history. The king was more strong-willed than his immediate prodecessors, and perhaps more lenient toward Christians and other minorities. This in turn earned him the epithet of 'Asim ("the Sinful") in the later Islamic sources (Tabari/Bosworth, 70), perhaps reflecting contemporary Zoroastrian feelings about his tolerance of Christians. Indeed, Christian sources from Rome (Procopius, 1.2, 8) consider him a noble soul and even a second Cyrus (McDonough, 2008; Shahbazi, "Yazdgerd I," *EIr*). Members of the nobility and the priesthood became his enemies due to his strong handed treatment of the Sasanian nobility and priesthood (Socrates Scholasticus, 7.8), although he seems to have survived their wrath. Instead, he was killed in a tragicomic manner by a kick from his horse! (Shahbazi, 2003). On his coins, he calls himself *Rām-Šahr* "[provider of] a calm realm," which might indeed be a reflection of his rule as a whole (Daryaee 2003). Yazdgerd's relatively long reign was also marked by a famous request from the Roman Emperor Arcadius to adopt the latter's son, the future Theodosios II, as his foster son (Agathias IV.26.6-7). Although the account of this event, recorded several decades later, was judged differently by later Byzantine historians (see Proc. *Wars* I.2.1-10), we can safely assume that it at least indicated a period of calm and mutual trust, or even reliance, between the two late antique empires.

Wahram V (r. 420-38 CE), a son of Yazdgerd I who resided at the Arab court of al-Hira, had to wrestle his crown from a usurper named Khosrow (Tabari/Bosworth, 90-93). He was obviously a successful king during whose reign the Sasanian realms enjoyed a period of prosperity, calm, and seemingly intense cultural production. Islamic sources greatly emphasize his connections to the city of Hira and its ruling family of the Nasrids (Fisher 2011). Of course, this is clearly a later literary device to legitimize the Nasrids and might even reflect the Hira origins of many of al-Tabari's accounts. On the other hand, it probably also reflects the truth, particularly the fact that the Arab clients of both the Sasanian and the Roman empires were becoming important players in the border skirmishes between these two powers.

Wahram's reign is highly romanticized in the Classical Persian literature, particularly in a great compendium of interrelated stories called *Haft Peykar* by the poet Nezami (12th century) whose fanciful stories might be drawing on actual Sasanian period romances. These stories include the coming of Indian minstrels known as *lur* (Koli, Roma, or Gypsies?) and the pleasure the king took in drinking and hunting. Wahram is commonly known by the epithet *Gur/Gōr (Jur* in Arabic sources: Tabari/Bosworth, 82), meaning "onager," presumably because of his love of hunting the animal. The story of his death is equally colorful, for it was said that while hunting in Māh (Media), Wahram fell into a marsh and disappeared (Daryaee 2008, 60-61). He was succeeded by his son, Yazdgerd II (r. 438-57 CE).

Yazdgerd II, unlike his namesake and grandfather, does not appear to have been very tolerant toward Christianity, at least in Armenia. The tale of the great rebellion of Vardan Mamikonian and its suppression at the battle of Avarayr by Mihr-Narse, Yazdgerd's vizier (attributed to Wahram V by al-Tabari: Tabari/Bosworth, 104-105), is recorded in the work of Armenian historian Elishe (Elishe/Thomson, 178ff.). It seems that for Yazdgerd and Mihr-Narse the control of Armenia meant a re-conversion of Armenians from Christianity to Zoroastrianism, making them part of a Zoroastrian *oecumene* designed to create a centralized Sasanian state. The defeat of the Mamikonian rebellion meant that *Persarmenia* – the majority of the Armenian territory under the Sasanian rule – was from this point on governed directly by the Sasanian court through a *Marzpan* (margrave) and was effectively incorporated into the Sasanian realm (Blockley, 1987). Yazdgerd's inclusion of the title of *kay* on his coins, a title originating from the Avesta, might also be indicative of a shift in Sasanian ideology away from *the King of (many) Kings* and more towards a divinely, or at least religiously, ordained *Great King*.

According to al-Tabari, the two sons of Yazdgerd II, Hormizd III (r. 457-9 CE) and Pēroz (r. 459-84 CE), ruled consecutively, although the latter deposed the former in a power struggle (Tabari/Bosworth, 107-109). During this confrontation, Caucasian Iberia (Georgia) gained independence and the eastern borders of the Sasanian Empire were laid open to attacks from the Hephthalites. Pēroz pacified Caucasian Albania and made an agreement with the Eastern Roman Empire to cooperate in defending the Caucasus from invaders (Pseudo-Joshua the Stylite 9-10) (Rapp 2014, pp. 182-183). This agreement compelled the Roman administration to pay a yearly supplement to the Sasanians for the upkeep of a defensive wall in the Caucasus, known as the Gate of Darband. The payment of this supplement was to have great consequences for the relations between the two empires and many of the wars in the sixth century.

In the east, however, Pēroz was much less successful. After initial campaigns on the northeastern frontiers of his domain, he was faced with great setbacks resulting in his capture by the Hephthalites in 469 CE. The Sasanians were forced to cede territory in the east, leave Prince Kavad as a hostage, and pay tribute to the Hephthalites, while Pēroz prepared for a second campaign. A second campaign in 484 to release Prince Kavad and take back the lost territories ended in a disastrous defeat in which Pēroz was killed and his army was decimated (Daryaee 2009, 25). A brother of Pēroz called Walakhsh/Walāsh (r. 484-8 CE) briefly managed to gain control and bring about relative calm, despite the empty treasury (Josh. Stylite 18). Walāsh's use of the title *Hu-Kay* ("the Good Kay/King") might be an indication of his claim to being a better ruler than his brother. He was, however, soon deposed in favor of Kavad I (r. 488-97, 499-531 CE), the son of Peroz who had spent his youth as a hostage in the Hephthalite court.

Needless to say, Kavad took over the empire in a state of chaos. The death of Pēroz had crushed the credibility of the Sasanians, particularly in the military sense. Territories in the east, including Bactria and Marv, were lost to the Hephthalites, and some of them would never again be recovered by the Sasanians. More importantly, the royal treasury was drained for the payment of war reparations to the Hephthalites. The abundance of the coinage of Kavad in Central Asia is a sign of this, and shows the great loss of wealth from the Sasanian territories.

Sources are quite scarce and confusing for this period of Kavad's reign. Procopius, Malalas, and Joshua the Stylite are our only contemporary sources, but the narrative of events is often formed by later, mainly Islamic sources and the hostile Zoroastrian ones. Likely as a result of the economic drain, and the inevitable social impact of military defeat and loss of wealth, a series of social upheavals appears to have taken place upon Kavad's succession to the throne. Latter sources attribute these to an individual named Mazdak, although it now seems quite established by the scholarship that the character of Mazdak belongs to the latter part of Kavad's reign (Crone, 1991). In any case, part of the social upheaval seems to have been blamed on Kavad himself, probably for attempting to undertake radical reforms, though possibly also for reducing or even confiscating the wealth of the nobility and the priestly class. The latter, in turn, removed and imprisoned the king, setting up his brother Zamasp (r. 497-9 CE) in his place (Tabari/Bosworth, 136). Zamasp's reign was short and seems to have been dominated by the nobility, although he issued coins during this period. Soon enough, Kavad was able to escape his prison and take refuge with his former hosts, the Hephthalites. In 499, with the assistance of the Hephthalites, he was able to remove Zamasp peacefully and reclaim his crown (Litvinsky, 1996: 140).

Kavad's second reign was a pivotal moment in Sasanian history and the point of origin for many of the characteristics of the latter Sasanian rule that survived its fall and helped form the mediaeval world, particularly in the Near East. His initial actions were to recover the military might of the Sasanians and to re-supplement the treasury. Roman building activities in the strategic city of Daras, near the border with Nisibis, and its elevation to the seat of a Dux provided this pretext. Kavad attacked Dara and set siege to Amida in 502-503 (Zacharias VII.3-4), demanding a halt to Roman fortification activities and a resumption of the payment for the defenses of the Caucasus, which emperor Anastasius had stopped (Josh. Stylite 20). Armenians too were encouraged by the hardline taken by the Romans against Kavad and rose again in rebellion, razing the fire-temple presumably built by Yazdgerd II (Josh. Stylite 21). The Armenian rebellion was quickly put down, but Kavad's new campaign against Rome was to dominate the Sasanian-Roman relations for most of the sixth century. It is in this period that the Sasanian failures in the east forced them to partially withdraw from Central Asia, a traditional sphere of involvement, and focus their attentions instead in the west, particularly on the control of Syria and Armenia. By 506, Kavad's campaign, including his seizure of Amida and Theodosiopolis, brought the Romans to the negotiating table. An uncertain agreement was reached, including a payment by the Romans, although there is no indication that the regular payments for the defenses of Caucasia were resumed (Procopius, *Wars*, I.9.24).

It must be after the treaty of 506 that Kavad embarked on his sociopolitical reforms. The aspects of these reforms are not clear and many were later attributed to his son, Khosrow I. However, they must have been less radical than what was passed during his first reign (Schindel 2013). A restructuring of the taxation system, organization of the Zoroastrian clerical administration, and a reforming of the nobility as well as the military appears to be the result of these reforms.

Later Islamic narratives compacted most of the rest of Kavad's story into the narrative of Mazdak and his rebellion, presented as a set of radical socio-religious reforms. Mazdak appears to have been a Zoroastrian priest who presented a particular reading of the scripture, emphasizing social justice and equality, something that was presented as communal sharing of women and wealth by the Zoroastrian and later Islamic accounts. Kavad's time, however, was most likely more occupied with policies in Transcaucasia, where in 521-522, a dispute over the kingdom of Lazica brought him into conflict with the Romans again, this time under Emperor Justin (Malalas, 17.9). Around 525, Kavad attempted a repeat of the adoption strategy of Arcadius and Yazdgerd I, proposing to Justin to adopt Kavad's son, Khosrow. The move was highly criticized by the Romans and was refused, even putting a newer perspective on the successful earlier case (Procopius, *Wars* I.11. 23-30). The new war also outlasted Kavad himself, who died in 531, amidst the fighting headed on the Roman side by a young Justinian and his famed general, Belisarius (Procopius, *Persian Wars* I-III).

Khosrow I Anusheruwan (r. 531-79) succeeded his old, seasoned father in a relatively stable period for the Sasanians. Despite the war with Byzantium, the Sasanians were enjoying a strong military, and their finances appear to have been in better shape than before. He is said to have killed Mazdak and his followers and to have thus "restored" the Zoroastrian order, although this might in fact be the time when Zoroastrian church structure was given its final form, creating a standard state Zoroastrianism which was to reflect the image of Sasanian Zoroastrianism as a whole (Rezakhani 2014).

Khosrow's reign marked an important juncture in Sasanian history. He is remembered as a wise and just ruler in both Persian and Arabic histories (Tabari/Bosworth, 146ff). Kavad I and Khosrow I together reorganized the Sasanian Empire and made it one of the strongest in the world in the sixth century CE. The reforms initiated by Kavad were continued and strengthened by Khosrow, and in fact are mostly credited to the latter (Rubin, 1995). Khosrow is also known for continuing the war with the Eastern Roman Empire of Justinian I, the details of which can be found in the famous work of Procopius (also see Dignas and Winter, 2001: 100-109). A famous treaty, concluded in 562 between the Roman and Sasanian Empires, tried to settle the state of affairs, but did not last long, although both empires at this point appear to be disinterested in continuing their wars as their interests lay elsewhere. Khosrow, indeed, was more interested in regaining the control of the east that was lost to his grandfather, Pēroz. In 570-571, an alliance between the Sasanians and the Khaganate of the Gök-Türks (or Western Turks) managed to destroy the central power of the Hephthalites and divide their territory. Sasanians gained control of the important border city of Marv, while the Turks added Bactria and much of Transoxiana to their territories. Following this, Khosrow also divided his territories into four military zones of the East, the West (or Azarbaigan), the South, and the North, each entrusted to a general (Gyselen 2001). This division, as well as the reforms mentioned above, shows a maturation of Sasanian administration and their confidence in their power, a clear trend in the late antique world.

Hormizd IV (r. 579-90 CE) appears to have been a less militaristic ruler than his ancestors, although his steadfastness in continuing their reforms bought him the hostility of his courtiers. Islamic sources such as Dinawari consider him a good and pious king who was interested in raising the status of the lower classes. This, in addition to his lack of attention to military affairs, indeed brought about his downfall through a palace coup. His son and successor, Khosrow II Aparwēz (r. 590-628 CE) (Tabari/Bosworth, 298-103), is considered the last great Sasanian Emperor.

Khosrow's succession did not go as smoothly as he might have hoped, since a general of his father rose in supposed revenge of Hormizd IV, forcing the young king to flee his capital of Ctesiphon. General Wahram Čobin ("Wooden") ran Khosrow out of the empire and crowned himself Wahram VI, the first time a non-Sasanian had claimed the throne, and an important indication of both the power of the military and the rising importance of the noble families of the empire, to one of which, *Mihran*, the general belonged. Khosrow in turn fled to the Eastern Roman Empire and sought the aid of Emperor Maurice (Tabari/Bosworth, 310-314). Maurice supplied mainly Armenian forces to Khosrow II, with which he managed to defeat Wahram – who fled to the court of the Turkic Khagan – and recapture his crown (Dignas and Winter, 236-240; Sebeos 76.8-18). A peace with the Romans was naturally concluded that spelled the end of all hostilities for the foreseeable future (Theophylact Sim. V.15.2). Khosrow then took revenge on those who had contributed to the murder of his father, although it is possible that he himself had a hand in that crime. A second rebellion by Wistahm, a maternal uncle of Khosrow and a conspirator in the removal of Hormizd, was soon put down, allowing the new king to establish his rule (Daryaee 2008, 85). Khosrow's policies after this point was to strengthen the basis of his power, particularly inside his territories, including clear lenience and patronage offered to the Christians of Mesopotamia and Khuzistan, from among whom he also chose a wife, Shirin (Theo. Sim. V.14.1-12).

In 602, however, a coup against Emperor Maurice resulted in the murder of the Roman Emperor and the usurpation of the throne by Phokas (Theo. Sim. VIII.15.2-7). Khosrow, claiming the presence of Maurice's son, Theodosius, in his court, thus embarked on a prolonged campaign against Rome in order to revenge the murder of Maurice (Dignas and Winter, 240-241). These campaigns resulted in the fall of Syria, Palestine, and Egypt, as well as significant portions of Anatolia into the hands of the Sasanians (Dignas and Winter, 115-115). The Sasanian general Shahin also managed to lay siege to Constantinople itself, which was ultimately unsuccessful. These gains in many senses marked the height of Sasanian power and the culmination of the dynasty's efforts at consolidating power and initiating socioeconomic reforms. For over twenty years, the Sasanians ruled over the eastern Mediterranean, threatening the very existence of the Eastern Roman Empire, the only remnant of the once mighty Mediterranean power.

Internal disputes over the prolonged war, as well as a successful counteroffensive by Heraclius, who by this time had managed to remove Phokas and re-organize the defenses of the empire, resulted in a reversal of fortunes in the mid 620s. By 628, not only were the territories in the Mediterranean realm restored to the Romans/Byzantines, but with the help of elements in the Sasanian court, the Roman emperor had also routed the Sasanian armies inside their own territories (Howard-Johnston, 1999). Khosrow was removed in a palace coup and his eldest son Shiroē was installed as Kavad II (628) (Dignas and Winter, 148-151). The very short reign of Kavad II was marked by internal chaos, as well as a major plague known by his name, the Plague of Shiroē, which had devastating demographic effects (Morony 2007).

The final phase of Sasanian rule was a period of factionalism and division within the empire, during which a number of kings came to power and were challenged by other distant members of the family of Sasan. Ardashir III (Sept. 628- Apr. 629), the son of Kavad II, was a child who was soon removed from the throne by one of the commanders of the war with Byzantium, Shahrbaraz. He in turn was toppled by the nobility who then installed Boran (628-630/31?), a daughter of Khosrow II (Emrani, 2009). Her rule was a period of consolidation of imperial power and rebuilding the empire. She was probably brought to the throne because she was the only legitimate heir. Another daughter of Khosrow II, Azarmigduxt (630-631?), replaced her sister. Boran and Azarmigduxt were deposed by another Sasanian general, and here we see that the military commanders were assuming more and more power in the face of the shaken monarchy, the competing nobility, and the Zoroastrian priests. Claimants such as Khosrow III or IV are also speculated mainly through numismatic evidence, before finally in 632, Yazdgerd III (632-651), grandson of Khosrow II, was installed on the throne (Shahbazi, "Sasanian Dynasty," *EIr.*).

Yazdgerd III's rule coincided with the conquest of the Sasanian Empire by the Muslims (Tyler-Smith, 2000). Starting in 637, the Muslim armies quickly managed to defeat the Sasanians in Qadisiyya, in southwestern Iraq, and soon in their capital at Ctesiphon. The last Sasanian king was forced to retreat to the east, from province to province, demanding loyalty and support from local populations. A second war against the Arabs ended disastrously with the defeat at Nihavand (642) and put an effective end to Sasanian imperial resistance. Finally, his dwindling forces were defeated by a coalition of local Persian and Hephthalite governors of Bactria. Tradition has it that Yazdgerd III was killed in 651 in Marv by a miller who did not recognize the king of kings.

The sons of Yazdgerd III fled further east, asking the Chinese Emperor Gaozong to aid them in their battle against the Muslims. For a time, Sasanian descendants continued to be recognized by the Chinese as legitimate holders of the Persian throne-in-exile and as governors of a "Persian Area Command" (*Bosi dudufu*) in Sistan. In the early eighth century CE, a Sasanian named Khosrow made a final, failed attempt to retake Iran from the Muslims, and this is the last time we hear of the family of Sasan (Compareti, 2009). The world of ancient Persia had come to an end and a new chapter in the history of the nation had begun. The grandeur of the kings, their wisdom and opulence, was emulated by the Muslim caliphs, and the name Khosrow, rendered as *Kisra*, became the general designation for a great ruler. The Sasanians also passed on the idea of *Eran*

("Iran") which held as a form of idealized territorial designation by dynasties from the Buyids to the Mongols, and was utilized effectively in the pre-Modern and Modern periods in order to form the modern nation-state.

# Sasanians and the East

Sasanian state strategy is commonly summarized in the concept of centralization. Since the beginning, historiography has put the Sasanian monarchy in stark contrast to the Arsacid one, coloring the former as a centralizing force as opposed to the decentralized structure of the latter (Shahbazi, 2005). The Arsacids, with their multi-layered system of power, are seen as the kings of many king(let)s, something that in the eyes of many, including early Islamic historians – who called them *Moluk ut-Tawayif* ("kings of clans") - made them weak and ineffective. Instead, the Sasanian founder Ardashir and his immediate successors are seen as forces of unity who coerced the different Arsacid/Hellenistic princedoms to submit to a centralized Sasanian power (Tabari/Bosworth, 8-16).

However, there are reasons to believe in the continuation of the Arsacid system at least in the first century of Sasanian rule, and perhaps beyond. Specifically, there appears to have been a continuation of the rule of minor princedoms, as well as perhaps a major kingdom, to the east of the Sasanian realm. The inscription of Shapur I at *Ka'ba-i Zardosht* (Huyse 1999) in Fars/Persis mentions several "kings," including the sons of Shapur I himself, who are counted as part of the court of the king of kings. An Arman Shah ("king of Armenia"), a Sakan Shah ("king of Sakas"), and a Meshan Shah ("king of Mesene") (in southern Iraq) are also quite prominent.

However, we possess, through numismatics, evidence

of the existence of a "dynasty" of Kushan Shahs ("kings of Kushan") in the region of Bactria and perhaps Gandhara in the east of the Sasanian territories and northern India. This dynasty, which can legitimately be considered a cadet branch of the Sasanians, appears to have ruled the territories of the great Kushan Empire. Minting coins from the Kushan capital of Bactra/Balkh, this dynasty mainly copied the style of Kushan gold coins, while the silver coin types were borrowed from the Sasanians (Brunner, 1974). The relationship between the kings of the dynasty and the Sasanians has not been ascertained and established, and the history of the dynasty is only known in a fragmentary manner and in almost absolute absence of written sources.

While the Kushan Shah dynasty, or the Kushano-Sasanians as they are sometimes called, are a direct manifestation of Sasanian interests in the eastern side of their empire, the involvement both predates them and also continues after the disappearance of this cadet branch. Indeed, from the beginning the Sasanians display strong interest, and possibly even roots, in the territories of the east. Ardashir's conquest of Merv is in fact a watershed moment in his career, as demonstrated by his coin types, while his conquest and destruction of the Indo-Parthian kingdom in Sistan appears to have been the moment of his precise claim to the title of the emperor/king of kings (Alram, 2007).

Shapur I might have been the king elevating the Kushano-Sasanians to their position, while Wahram III is called the King of Sakas by Narseh in his Paikuli inscriptions. During the reign of Shapur II, the "Huns," moving south and west from the Inner Asian steppe, threatened the Sasanian borders in the east, and possibly put an end to the Kushano-Sasanian rule (Göbl, 1967). However, a confrontation leading to peace brought a Hunnic contingent, headed by king Grumbates, to the Sasanian army in the wars with the Roman Empire (Amm. Marc. 16.9).

The relief of Shapur II and his brother Ardashir II at *Taq-e Bostan* too might betray the existence of an eastern connection in the Sasanian court (Tanabe, 1985). The god under whose auspices the treaty between the two brothers is being concluded is Mithra, the god of contracts and treaties (Kaim, 2009). Both the god, as well as the lotus over which he stands, have been iconographically connected to eastern Iran, particularly the territory of the Kushans, leading to the suggestion that Ardashir II might have acted as a Kushan Shah prior to his accession.

Bactria and Transoxiana at this time, however, were being controlled by the aforementioned Hunnic forces, particularly a clan best known under the name of their ruler, Kidara. (Errington and Curtis, 85-86) The coins of Kidarite rulers are a direct copy of Kushano-Sasanian (and by extension, Sasanian) silver issues, using the Pahlavi script, in a clear case of connection to the Sasanian court and administration (Zeimal, 1996).

Kidarites and their immediate successors known as the Alkhan (Grenet 2002, 210) were pushed over the Hindu-Kush towards Gandhara by a new tribal grouping called the Hephthalites (Sunderman, 1996; Rahman et. al., 2006). It is with the Hephthalites that we start a period of intense Sasanian engagement with eastern Iran and Central Asia. The Hephthalites, known sometimes by the contemporary Byzantine sources as the White Huns, were probably a new tribal confederacy made up of several already settled "Hunnic" tribes. They appear to have enjoyed a relatively centralized administrative system headed by a king, and surely a very organized army. During the second half of the fifth century, Hephthalites formed the largest threat to Sasanian dominance, controlling not only Bactria, but also apparently parts of southern Transoxiana and borders of the Sasanian realm in the northeast. The Sasanian emperor Peroz indeed undertook several campaigns against the Hephthalites, having to pay heavy tributes to them after his defeats, before being killed in a war against the Hephthalite king Akhshunwar (sometimes Khushnawaz in Classical Persian accounts) in 484 CE. Kavad I, Peroz's son, was left as a hostage with the Hephthalites, and later when removed from the throne in the Mazdakite revolt, again took refuge with the Hephthalites.

It appears that from the second half of the fifth century onwards, the Sasanians lost effective control of Bactria, the core territory of the Kushans and Kushano-Sasanians. This might be the reason for an increasing attention to the west of their empire and the prolonged wars with the Romans in the sixth century. It also will clearly explain the need for deep socioeconomic reforms in the Sasanian realm, since the royal treasury must have been fully bankrupt after the payment of hefty ransoms and tributes to the Hephthalites following the death of Peroz (Sarkhosh-Curtis, 1999). As a result, we hear little of eastern Iran in the sixth century from a Sasanian point of view. Bactria and Zawulistan appear to have been consolidated into the Hephthalite state, while Transoxiana, namely Sogdiana, was left on its own to thrive. The Sogdian trade network, quite important in the economy of sixth- to eighth-century China and the Middle Eastern world, was mostly developed during this period (de la Vaissière, 2005).

The Sasanians started acting to regain their dominance in the east around 558. Their actions were in concert with the advances of the Gok-Türk/Western Turk empire (Harmatta, 1996). In fact, we know from Byzantine sources that a Turk Khaqan named *Silzaboulos* advanced his armies against Transoxiana and Bactria at this time, while the Sasanian Khosrow I also attacked the Hephthalites from the south and the west. The Byzantine accounts of campaigns of Silzaboulos are corroborated by the report of Gok- Türk advancements under Khaqan *Sinjibu* in Chinese sources, as well as in the

Orkhon inscription (Sinor, 1990). The Sasanians appear to
have regained the important city of Marv and possibly parts of
Sogdiana, while the Gok-Türk became masters of Bactria, most
of Sogdiana, and Khwarazmia. This campaign indeed might be
the same one in which Wahram Čobin, the future rebel, made
his name, and his friendship with the Gok-Türk Khaqan is
evident through the tale of his refuge at the court of the Khaqan
following his defeat by Khosrow II and his Byzantine army
supporters (Tabari/Bosworth, 315-316).

The last glaring episode of Sasanian involvement with
east Iran is the terminal period of their rule, when Yazdgerd
III flees towards Transoxiana, hoping to gather support in the
area. While the local rulers appear to have been uninterested,
it is in fact Transoxiana and Bactria that provided the refuge
for the fleeing Persians at the end. In the documents of Mt.
Mugh, the mountain fortress of Dewashtich, the last king of
Sogdiana, one comes across the mention of a Persian general.
Dewashtich, protecting himself from the Muslim armies in 724
CE, was seeking support from anywhere he could, including
the Chinese. While his agent the Afshun/Afshin was busy
betraying him, a Persian general, presumably with an army,
was at a reasonable distance, trying to reach Mt. Mugh and
Dewashtich. Resistance, however, proved futile for Dewashtich,
but Sogdiana might have represented the last viable refuge for
the remaining Sasanian armies resisting the Islamic conquests
(Grenet & de la Vaissiere, 2002). Additional resistance was
offered up the early ninth century further south in Sistan and
Zabulistan, namely by a family of rulers known as Rutbil in the
Islamic sources (Bahar, Tarikh-e Sistan) whose endurance and
heroism might have been partially responsible for engendering
the Rostam myth-cycle.

Figure.8. Coins of Hormizd I Kushanshah

# Ideology, Empire, and Glory

The most important aspect of Sasanian rule was in fact the realization of an imperial ideology that was implemented through the imposition of the old Iranian worldview contained in the Zoroastrian sacred text, the *Avesta*. Without this, there would simply have been no reason for establishing an empire by Ardashir I (224-240 CE), or for its Afro-Asiatic overexpansion during the reign of Khusro II (590-628 CE), which caused its eventual . In a sense, ideology was the driving force for the Sasanians and the *rasion d'être* for what came to be called *Iranshahr* or the "Empire of the Iranians." This vision of *Iranshahr* or its truncated form Iran was an invention of the Sasanians that did not exist in the preceding Arsacid or Achaemenid Empires. This invention is manifest from the fact that neither before the Sasanians nor after their demise at the hands of the Muslims did their neighbors call this territory as such, and instead used the traditional designation of *Persia*, *Fars*, or *Persis*. The idea of *Iranshahr* came with religious and ideological trappings that necessitated the unification of locations associated with Iranian habitation. This complex construction of an imperial ideology, with the notion of kingship, religion, and a territory, was based on the Hellenistic, Mesopotamian, and Iranian worldviews, combined together with the local tradition of the Persian lords in the province of Fars (Daryaee 2014, 12).

By the fifth and the sixth centuries CE the Sasanian

family, namely the sons of the king of kings, kept the empire together through a sophisticated bureaucracy, as evidenced by the sigilographic and numismatic evidence (Gyselen, 1989). Beyond the Iranian Plateau, the Sasanian Empire, the self-designated "Empire of the Iranians" (*Iranshahr*), was centered at Ctesiphon in Mesopotamia. In a sense the "Heart of *Iranshahr*," as the medieval Muslim geographers called it, was Mesopotamia – the Sasanian province of *Surestan* – a fact that demonstrated the influence of the old Near Eastern tradition on the newly found Sasanian Empire. The new empire was cognizant of the history and heritage of the lands it had come to rule over.

This new empire, however, was maintained and controlled through the institution of kingship, which was not static in the four centuries of its existence; based on internal constraints and requirements, the ruler's role was continually redefined, ranging from that of a divine king to that of a *cosmokrator* (Panaino, 2009). Among the most important ideas were the Zoroastrian notions of Iranian kingship, which served in the takeover of land and in territorial battles, and was later significantly developed to fit the realities of the late antique world. This Iranian king with his or her attributes was tied to the concept of *Iranshahr*, and one could not survive without the other.

*Xwarrah* or "Glory" (Lubotsky, 1998) is central to the ancient Iranian royal ideology as demonstrated in the *Avesta*, and is a prerequisite of rightful rule in the *Avesta*. In the Avestan Yašts one encounters the Kayanid kings battling the enemies of the Iranians and those who seek to gain sovereignty over the Iranian lands. To gain this rule, every one of the rightful Kayanid rulers, those before them, and the seekers of power make sacrifices to deities to be granted the *xwarrah*. The *xwarrah* is granted or withheld from the Iranian rulers and the false non-Iranian evil characters based on the judgment of the gods. In Iranian art the *xwarrah* or glory was depicted usually with a halo around the king's head, and this also appeared in Sasanian art (Soudavar 2003). In later Persian literature and starting with Ferdowsi, the composer of the *Book of Kings* (*Shahnameh*) based on the Sasanian *Khoday-namag* (*Book of Lords*), the concept was further elaborated and came to be used by the medieval Muslim dynasties on the Iranian Plateau and in Central Asia to legitimize their rule. As in the *Avesta* and with the Kayanids, the Sasanian family claimed the royal "Glory" (*xwarrah*). The symbol at times appeared with the king as a ram or with specific insignias associated with the family of Sasan. Of course *xwarrah* was bestowed by Ohrmazd and other deities such as Lady Anahita on the king of kings in the form of a diadem in the royal rock reliefs (Daryaee, 2014, 18).

Through fire-temples and instructions to the Zoroastrians throughout the empire, this idea was made current and accepted. For others the idea was understood through the silver gilded dishes demonstrating the awesome king in banquet, hunting, or battle scenes. For those who were able to come to the court, such as foreign ambassadors, the immense crown suspended from a vault that mimicked the cosmos suggested the importance of the king of kings in the universe. The image of Khusro on his coinage also placed the king with four stars and crescents on the four sides, suggesting that the king of kings of *Iranshahr* was the king of the four corners of the world. Indeed in such royal imagery, *Iranshahr* was the center of the world.

The sanctity of the King of Kings and his importance for the well-being of the empire was paramount for the imperial ideology. Islamic sources mention that when an audience was given to see the king, he was usually hidden behind a veil, as he was not to be seen by all. He was like the sun and the moon, and held the same importance. Only during specific times in the year did the king make a public appearance. For example, during the *Nowruz* (New Year) and *Mihregan* (autumn) celebrations, gifts were exchanged and the king made speeches to the public. These annual ceremonies were held so that the cosmic order and the order of the universe and the empire could be maintained through the appearance of the king of kings, which ensured abundance, peace, and the well-being of the empire (Daryaee, 2014, 19-20). From the sixth century, the well-being of the king of kings was so important that he did not participate in wars as his loss would have symbolically meant the loss of the glory and hence the well-being of *Iranshahr* (Whitby 1994).

Figure. 9. Shapur II with Mithra glowing with Xwarrah at Taq-e Bustan

# Economy and Trade

As for most ancient and mediaeval civilizations, Sasanian economy was greatly dependent on agriculture, both sowing and animal husbandry. The Sasanian territories, however, included great swaths of land that suffered from very low precipitation, possibly with the exception of Khuzistan and Mesopotamia/ Surestan. While Mesopotamia, Sasanian *Surestan*, enjoyed an ancient agricultural tradition and relatively reliable sources of water, the Iranian Plateau was made up of hilly ground and suffered from an acute lack of rain (P. Christensen, 1996, Ch. 6). As such, agriculture appears to have been highly localized and concentrated in certain areas. Surestan and Khuzestan possessed fertile land and semi-reliable water. Traditionally, these areas had been used for grain production, as well as limited horticulture (mostly dates).

Large irrigation projects by the Sasanian administration, whose evidence survive in both literary and archaeological records, must have been a conscious attempt at remedying the problem. The large canal of Nahruwan was a famed project in southern Mesopotamia, while smaller irrigation systems were also founded in northern Mesopotamia, allowing for increased settlement in the upper reaches of the Diyala River (Adams, 1965: 89-99). We are not well aware of the function of the complex system of canals and drop-towers in Shushtar, but their agricultural and possibly industrial function seem to be indisputable. Similar structures in Deh Luran appear to function as watermills, used for processing local agricultural production (Neely 1974: 39-40).

Recent research shows that the Sasanian state invested heavily in these areas, creating hydraulic systems for irrigation, possibly with the aim of utilizing marginal land (Wenke, 1975: 200ff; Neely, 1974: 42). It has additionally been suggested that with the introduction of new crops, mostly cotton and sugar cane, these areas were made commercially important (Bulliet, 2011). Our information for agriculture on the Iranian Plateau is patchy, due to limited textual evidence and the paucity of archaeological surveys. It seems that whenever it was possible to create irrigation systems such as *Karez/Qanats* (underground aqueducts), agriculture was heavily practiced. An example of this is on the Damghan plain in north-central Iran, where the irrigation resulted in intensive settlements around the central plain, before they retreated to mountain valleys and switched production to horticulture (Trinkaus, 1985). The rest of the plateau, judging from its terrain and later sources, was heavily involved in transhumant cattle-raising and animal husbandry.

In trade, the Sasanians competed with the Romans over silk, and they disputed trade as far away as Sri Lanka. There was a Sasanian colony in Malaysia that was composed of merchants. Persian horses were shipped to Ceylon, and a Persian colony was established on that island, where ships came from Persia to its port. By the sixth century it appears that the Persians were not only bent on controlling the Persian Gulf and the Arabian Sea, but also looked farther east, which brought them into conflict with Rome. Silk appears to have been an important commodity desired by the Romans, and they sought to circumvent Persian traders to get lower prices. Consequently, the Byzantines had to seek the aid of the Christian Ethiopians, who were expelled by the Yemenis with the backing of the Sasanians in that region.

The Sasanian domains seem to have been in active trade

relations with China. Imported objects, such as Tang dynasty export wares, and other items from Rome, were found at the port of Siraf (Whitehouse and Williamson, 1973). Trade with China was conducted through two avenues, one being the famous Silk Road (see Rezakhani 2010 for a critique), and the other being the sea route (Daryaee 2003). This maritime trade became more important because of the political situation, and ports in Persis/ Fars became increasingly central to this trade (Whitehouse and Williamson, 1973).

Off the coast of China there have been finds of Sasanian coins, which again suggest the importance of maritime trade between this region and Persia. At least three sites where Sasanian coins have been found along the southeast coast of China make it probable that ships from the Persian Gulf came there. These are the sites of Kukogng, Yngdak, and Suikai, which had connections with trade in the Persian Gulf. Many of the coins belong to the late fifth through seventh centuries CE, which again attests to the importance of the Persian Gulf in the late Sasanian period.

As for domestic commerce, we rely on the seals and bullae that give some insight into the Sasanian administrative institutions (Gyselen 2007). In terms of commercial activity, we can tell that there was a vibrant domestic exchange based on finds of bullae and seals bearing the names of cities in the districts of the province of Persis/Fars. The bullae were used to seal packages destined for maritime or caravan trade, which is supported by later historical evidence. It is also important to note that bullae finds in South Asia, especially in Mantai in Sri Lanka, attest to Persian economic activity there as well.

Trade was conducted by companies and religious communities who combined their resources and formed partnerships. The term used for joint partnership in the Middle Persian legal texts is *hambayih*, which really meant holder of a common share whose joint investment would have brought a better return and a larger purchasing power. (Choksy 1988) These joint partnerships were probably based on religious association as well, where Zoroastrians created their own *hambayih* but may have dealt with other religious groups outside their regional reach.

We are well informed with regard to the legal aspects of trade and business agreements. Drafts of agreements were drawn up, signed, and sealed, and a copy was kept at the local office of registry, *diwan*. These agreements were legally binding, and depending on the violation, the accused was brought before a lesser or higher magistrate who was also a high ranking priest.

The principle commercial activity in the city was performed by the merchants (*wazarganan*) who were from the hutukhshašan estate. Commerce (*wazarganih*) was conducted in the bazaar (*wazar*), which today remains the economic center of small and large cities in Iran. As with today's markets, it appears that each group of artisans occupied a specific section (Persian *raste*) of the bazaar. A list of various professions who occupied special places in the bazaar included blacksmith, iron-molder, silversmith, silver-molder, roof-maker, string-maker, "Blacksmith," tailor, dressmaker, porcelain pot-maker, carpenter, washerman, shoemaker, shoemaker of a kind of shoe made of strings, potter, baker, book-painter, painter, cup-maker, tanner, ironsmith, dyer, various builders, barber, tent-maker, cooks who prepared sweets and finger foods, tablecloth-maker, goldsmith, and saddler.

There were other professions, but we are not sure if they were in the bazaar or not. Each artisan (*kirrog*) guild was headed by a head of the guild (*kirrogbed*). The activity and the prices of the bazaar were overseen by a head of the bazaar (*wazarbed*) who probably represented the artisan class. It was in these centers where local products were produced and commodities from other provinces as well as some of the foreign products entered the cities via the caravans (*karwan*). These caravans were led by a caravan leader (*sartwa*) who was either hired by the merchant or was in joint business with him.

While barter system was in use at the local level in villages and the like, the Sasanians brought about a standardization of weights and the minting of coinage which was directed from above and under the control of the imperial administration. The most common type of Sasanian coins were silver (*drahm*), one-sixth silver (*dang*) and copper coins (*pashiz*) used for local daily transaction. Gold was only minted ceremonially and does not appear to have been in circulation for trade and exchange. While the increase in the use of copper and bronze coinage in certain parts of the empire attests to the increase in trade and governmental control, the silver coinage was much more prevalent. On the obverse of these we find the portrait of the King of Kings along with a name and title, such as "Ardashir King of Kings of Iran, who is from the race of the Gods." On the reverse of the coinage is a fire altar sometimes alone and sometimes with two attendants flanking the fire. Until the late fifth century CE the coins did not indicate their mints, which makes it difficult to determine the number of mints and amount of production at each location. While there are more than one hundred mint-marks known, no more than twenty were producing the majority of the coins in the empire.

Figure. 10. Seal impression of a Zoroastrian priest from Shiraz

# Religion

The Sasanian rule is most associated with Zoroastrianism (Kreyebroek 2013), the ancient Iranian religion with close connections to the religion reflected in the Indian *RigVeda*. Although our sources tell us about Zoroastrianism from the late Sasanian period, it is generally understood that the religion enjoyed wide adherence in Iran from the ancient period, but certainly from the Arsacid times. Ardashir, the founder of the Sasanian dynasty, is given strong religious connections in historiography, and his grandfather and the eponymous ancestor of the dynasty, Sasan, is said to be a priest of the goddess Anahid/Anahita in Istakhr. The coins of Ardashir and his descendants up to the fifth century bare the phrase "… who is descended from the gods" on their obverse, while the reverse displays a fire altar, most closely associated with Zoroastrianism (Alram/Gyselen, 2003).

The famous inscriptions of Kerdir, the chief priest of Wahram II, are our best evidence for the state of religion in the early Sasanian period. In them, Kerdir chronicles his own rise to the position of the chief Mobed of Zoroastrianism, and at the same time mentions his persecution and purging of the adherents of other religions, including Buddhists, Jews, Christians, and Manichaeans (McKenzie, 1989). Despite this harsh depiction, early Sasanian kings appear to be rather tolerant toward other religions and even positively accommodating toward them. Shapur I in fact allows Mani, the prophet of

Manichaeism, to freely preach and convert, and the prophet writes a book in Middle Persian, named *Shapuragan*, in his honor. Mani was similarly favored by Hormizd I and Wahram I, while the ascendance of Kerdir under Wahram I finally caused the downfall of Mani and a general extradition and execution of his followers.

Christianity also was accommodated in the Sasanian territories (Payne 2015), although it was occasionally persecuted under various kings. The reason, particularly after Constantine and Theodosius I, was the fear of the Sasanian administration from the Christian community and their partiality toward the Christian empire of Rome. The efforts of Yazdgerd II and his chancellor Mihr-Narseh in the fifth century in converting Armenians to Zoroastrianism should also be treated in the same vein (Thomson, 1982). This fear, however, decreased after the Council of Chalcedon in 451, when the internal disagreements caused the flight of many "Eastern" Christians to the Sasanian territories and the formation of a native, independent Christian community in the Sasanian territories. Eventually under Khosrow I, Hormizd IV, and Khosrow II, this community established itself in the Sasanian realm, created a central patriarchal seat in Ctesiphon, as well as local bishoprics as far east as Darab in Fars/Persis and Marw in the northeast (McCullough, 1982: 157-162). Members of this church were also responsible for the spread of Christianity in Central Asia and its transportation to Turko-Mongolian tribes of Inner Asia via the Sogdian trade network.

Jews had lived in the Sasanian territories, particularly in southern Mesopotamia, since the Achaemenid period. Headed by a Resh Galota "leader of the exiles," these Jews were engaged in agricultural activities, artisanal production, and commerce, as is recorded in the Talmud (Mokhtarian 2015). The greater part of the document, in fact, was composed and compiled during the Sasanian period, forming the larger of the two Talmuds known as the Babylonian Talmud or the Bavli. Based on its testimony, the Jewish community enjoyed an autonomy in legal and judicial terms, possibly providing a glimpse of Sasanian official policies toward minorities (Secunda, 2013).

Starting in the fifth century, the Zoroastrian establishment gained more power in the Sasanian court. This is evident from Yazdgerd II's campaigns against Armenians, from the proliferation of devotional literature addressed towards creating "orthodoxy," and finally from the successful purge of the Mazdakites following the removal of Kavad I from the throne in 494. The Zoroastrian church, in unity with the Sasanian nobility, became the official religious profession of the government. During the course of the sixth and seventh centuries, judging from the proliferation of seals and bullae attesting to this, more and more governmental positions were bestowed on low to high ranking Zoroastrian clergy. In particular, the administration of legal contracts, from sales and shipping of goods to land purchase, were witnessed by various *Dastwars* and *Hirbeds*. The role of social justice and provisions for the good were entrusted to a particular cleric bearing the title of "Judge and Protector of the Needy" (Daryaee, 2001), and indeed, the *Mobedan Mobed* (the Great Priest) enjoyed high prestige and influence. This is, evidently, the status quo that left a lasting impression on the minds of early Islamic historians, both Muslim and Zoroastrian, and by extension modern historians, imagining the whole of the Sasanian period as a period of "theocracy" and dominance of a rigid Zoroastrian church.

Probably as a way of rebelling against this slowly establishing status quo, Mazdak, himself a Zoroastrian priest, instigated a rebellion in the late fifth century. Mazdakism is presented exclusively through hostile accounts, whether in contemporary Byzantine sources (Procopious or Joshua the Stylite) or in later Muslim (Shahristani, Dinawari) and Zoroastrian (Denkard) accounts. The universal accusation is a charge of "communal sharing," mostly framed as "sharing of wives" and thus sexual promiscuity, but also as the sharing of property and wealth. Modern historians, often influenced by 20th-century Marxist idealism, have imagined Mazdakism as an ideal "proto-Communism" and re-casted the Sasanian efforts at eliminating the cult as a classic class-struggle (Rezakhani, 2014). Whatever the truth might be, it seems certain that Mazdakism was only one reflection of a wider socioeconomic and cultural movement in Sasanian society that was translated through a religious prism. The ideas and ideals that at one time were reflected in Mazdakism did not cease to exist and appeared in different shapes and forms and under various rubrics in the early Islamic period.

Figure. 11. Kerdir the Chief Zoroastrian Priest

# Language and Literature

The official, or at least the most widespread, language of the Sasanian realm was Middle Persian, a language native to the province of Fars/Persis in the southern Iranian Plateau (Sundermann, 1989). The earliest major written source available from inside the empire itself is Shapur I's *Ka'ba-i Zardosht* inscription (ŠKZ). The inscription is carved in Middle Persian, Parthian, and Greek, reflecting the three linguistic traditions of the time: the contemporary reality, the immediate past, and the classical Hellenistic (Rubin, 2002). Soon after, we have an inscription from Shapur the son of Hormizd, a grandson of Shapur I, who was styled the King of Sakas (Daryaee, 1380/2001). His lapidary inscription, on a column in Persepolis, is in Middle Persian only, something that perhaps is justifiable by its unofficial tone and setting, carved over the course of a short camping. Narseh, the son of Shapur I who claimed the crown for himself in 293, in turn, left us a major inscription, however damaged, in Paikuli, south of modern Sulaimaniya in the Iraqi Kurdistan. Here, Narseh uses only Middle Persian and Parthian, having abandoned the Greek. Both ŠKZ and Paikuli are in the genre of official proclamations and victory literature and are quite formulaic. But both do betray a well-developed literary style, reflecting that Middle Persian was not a completely new language for the composition of literature and official declarations.

We have very little inscription after this point. Most of our written sources from the Sasanian period appear to have been composed in the fifth to seventh centuries and committed to writing in the late Sasanian and early Islamic periods. However, it is fair to assume that many of these were simply compilations of earlier compositions whose latest manuscripts are simply those that have reached us. Here, the evidence of the creation in the late Sasanian period of the Avestan script, based on the Middle Persian Pahlavi script (Weber, 2007), is itself proof of the proliferation of the use of the latter. Surely the widespread use of written Pahlavi led to the well-known realization that it is highly inefficient for accurate transmission of the complicated Avestan sound system and even more importantly, the sacred contents of the Avesta, the Zoroastrian holy book (Stausberg, 1998: 258-263).

Interest in literature and a need for recording the past also gave incentives in the fifth and sixth centuries to a movement for composition of new pieces, as well as translations from other languages. It is often posited that the rule of Khosrow I saw the beginning of the compilation of the historical genre known as *Khuday-namag* ("the Book of the Lords"), which in various texts reflected the mythical and historical tales of the history of the kings of Iran. This essentially acted as the source material for the history of pre-Islamic Iran for Muslim historians such as al-Tabari, as well as for the great Persian epic, the *Shahnameh* of Ferdowsi. Alongside the Khuday-namag texts, other epics, romances, and pieces of devotional poetry were also composed, some of which, including *Ayadgar-i Zareran*, have reached us in original form, while others like *Vis o Ramin* are known through New Persian translations and compositions. At the same time, serious works such as *Mādayān-ī Hazār Dādestān* ("the Book of a Thousand Judgments"), a compilation of legal rulings and commentary, were composed and probably finalized in the seventh century (Macuch, 1993). However, the largest body of Sasanian works of literature are the commentaries on the Avestan, the Zoroastrian holy scripture, which were composed in Middle Persian. Written either in the Pahlavi or the Avestan script, these texts (called Zand and Pazand, respectively, based on the script) formed a large body of works that continued well into the Islamic period and constitutes essentially the vast majority of what we have in Middle Persian (Boyce 1968 : Macuch 2009). Last but not least were the translations from other languages, most importantly Indic languages (either Sanskrit or Prakrit), such as *Panchatantra* (de Blois, 1990). Although the original translations have not survived, we know from Islamic sources such as *Al-Fihrist* of Ibn Nadim that these works were brought into the Sasanian world by travelers such as Borzoe the Physician who is also credited with translating the work to Middle Persian. These Middle Persian translations were then used in the early Abbasid period for translations into Arabic, resulting, in the case of *Panchatantra*, in the great collection of fables known as *Kalila wa Dimna*.

Middle Persian and Avestan, however, were not the only languages used for literature. Aramaic, in both Iraqi and Syriac forms, was the vehicle for widespread composition of texts in the Sasanian period. The Babylonian Talmud was composed in Aramaic mostly during the Sasanian period in southern Iraq/Surestan, and represents a major work of late antique literature and legal composition (Secunda, 2009). Syriac was the language of the Church of the East, centered in Ctesiphon, and the language in which church histories, local monastic histories, and even chronicles were composed by the Syriac Christians (Brock, 1997). In the east, Bactrian was the official language, a remnant of Kushan dominance, and was used widely for the composition of legal documents, and presumably for literature as well, although little of the latter remains beyond fragmentary Buddhist texts (Sims-Williams,

2008). Sogdian, the great language of trade in Central Asia as far east as China, was a native of Sogdiana, the regions of Bukhara and Samarqand in Transoxiana. It was used as a major vehicle for the transmission of religious texts of the Manichaean and Christian communities of Central Asia, resulting in a rich religious literature that includes many fables and anecdotes, as well as translations of texts such as the Psalms. Incidentally, the oldest Avestan manuscript we have in our possession is a copy of the well-known Zoroastrian prayer Ashem Vohu written in the Sogdian script (Rose, 2011: 151-152)!

Figure. 12. Ostraca from Hamedan

# Postscript

The Sasanian Empire was one of the major forces of the late antique world. Often represented as the "adversary" of the Roman Empire in the east, and thus on its "periphery," the Sasanian Empire was in fact the center of a prolific sociocultural, political, and economic sphere that became widespread following its conquest by the Muslims. Political centralization, robust and expanding economy, socio-religious innovations and changes, and growing cultural activities made the Sasanians the blueprint for subsequent polities in the region. Often under-researched, many aspects of Sasanian culture and society are left unknown, and thin connections are made via shallow evidence for such influences. The emerging evidence and the development of more sophisticated studies of the period would no doubt show the centrality of the Sasanians in the late antique world, and asses their lasting legacy in the history of West and Central Asia until the modern times.

Figure. 13. Stucco from Seymareh

# A Timeline of Late Antique Iran

Figure. 14. Jousting scenes at Naqsh-e Rustam

# Timeline

(all dates are AD)

214: Speculated date of the start of the rebellion of Pābag and his sons against the local ruler of Persis (al-Tabari's *Juzihr*).

216: the Roman Emperor Caracalla invades the Arsacid Empire; captures Nisibis.

216: Possible date of succession of Artabanus IV to the Arsacid throne.

216: Possible date of the birth of prophet Mani.

217: Caracalla is assassinated near Carrhea by his bodyguard.

Ca. 222: Ardashir becomes the main Sasanian contender. Establishes his power in *Gur* (*Ardashir-Khurrah*, NP *Firuzabad*) in southern Persis.

224: Ardashir wins the *Battle of Hormizdagan* against Artabanus IV; is crowned in Ctesiphon as the King of Kings (MP *Shahanshah*)

226: Ardashir defeats Vologases VI, the last Arsacid ruler in Media.

226-240: Ardashir invades and conquers central Iran, Marw, and Sistan, removing Farn-Sasan, the last Indo-Parthian ruler.

241: Ardashir abdicates the throne in favour of his son, Shapur I.

241-242: Shapur captures Nisibis and Carrhae; opposed by Gordian III.

244: Shapur defeats, and possibly kills, Gordian III in the *Battle of Misikhe* (thereafter *Piruz-Shapur/Anbār*).

244: Philip the Arab, the successor of Gordian III, concludes a peace treaty, paying homage and leaving Armenia under Sasanian control.

245-250: Campaigns of Shapur in the east, possible end to Kushan control in Bactria.

252: Khosrov II of Armenia, from the Arsacid/Arshakuni house, is murdered; Shapur appoints his son Hormizd-Ardashir as the "Great King of Armenia".

256: Shpur captures and sacks Antioch-on-the-Orontes.

257: the Roman Emperor Valerian launches his campaigns in Syria, opposing Shapur.

260: Valerian is defeated and captured by Shapur at the *Battle of Edessa*; possibly dies in Sasanian captivity.

Ca. 260-261: Approximate date of the carving of the famous inscription of *Shapur at Naqsh-i Rustam* (ŠKZ) in Persis, near Staxr.

260-270: Peace in the Sasanian Empire. Construction of the city of Bishapur as the monumental residence of Shapur I.

270: Hormizd I ascends the Sasanian throne. The height of the activities of *Mani*, the founder of *Manichaeism*.

271: Wahram I succeeds his brother Hormizd I.

273: Zenobia, the Queen of Palmyra and brieflz the strongest power in Syria, is defeated by the Roman emperor Aurenlian with the compliance of Wahram I.

274: Wahram I executes Mani at the instigation of the Zoroastrian priest, Kerdir.

274: Wahram II succeeds his father Wahram I. Kerdir is rewarded with high honours.

274-282: Conflicts in Sistan and Khurasan.

282: Roman Emperor Carus launches an invasion of Mesopotamia.

283: Wahram II recaptures Mesopotamia and expels Carus.

286: Emperor Diocletian invades Mesopotamia.

287: Tiridates declares himself the independent ruler of Armenia.

290-295: Possible start of the rule of the Sasanian cadet branch, the Kushano-Sasanians (*Kushanshahs*) in the former Kushan territories of Bactria and Arachosia, later to expand into Gandhara.

293: The minster Wahnām installs Wahram III *Sakanshah*, "King of the Sakas," to replace Wahram II (possibly his father?).

293: Narseh, son of Shapur I and the Great King of Armenia, invades western Iran and removes Wahram III; builds the monument of *Paikuli* and orders the carving of his famous inscription on it.

296: Narseh attacks and removes Tiridates III from the throne of Armenia.

298: Galerius, Caesar in the East, defeats Narseh in the *Battle of Satala* and captures his wife and other royal personages.

298-299: Peace treaties result in recovery of Narseh's household, restoration of Tiridates to the throne of Armenia. Nisibis is established as the border post between Rome and the Sasanians.

301: The traditional date for the conversion of Tiridates III to Christianity.

302: Hormizd II replaces his father Narseh.

309: Guards assassinate Hormizd II and install his son, Adur-Narseh, on the throne.

309: Adur-Narseh is assassinated; the throne passes on to the infant Shapur II.

ca. 326-330?: Shapur's early campaigns against the Arab tribes who had invaded the southern Persian coast during his minority; receives the title of *Dhul-Aktaf*, "the One with (broad?) Shoulders; the one who owns shoulders."

337-350: Shapur's campaigns against Rome, without much result.

ca. 350: Chionites (Huns?) invade Bactria and destroy the Kushano-Sasanians.

358: Renewal of hostilities between Shapur II and Constantine II.

359: Shapur II puts Amida under siege; the Chionite king *Grumbates* is reported to be present in the Sasanian army along with his son.

362: the Roman Emperor Julian "the Apostate" invades Mesopotamia from the direction of Carrhae and proceeds almost as far as Ctesiphon.

363: Julian is assassinated by his own troops. Jovian concludes a treaty with Shapur II and gives up Nisibis to the Sasanian control.

Ca. 365: Possible date of the relief of Shapur II at *Taq-e Bostan*.

379: Shapur II dies, ending the longest reign in Sasanian (and Iranian) history.

379: Ardashir II succeeds his brother on the throne; most of his reign is occupied with the affairs in Armenia.

383: Shapur III, the son of Shapur II, ascends the Sasanian throne.

384: A treaty is concluded between Shapur III and Theodosius I, dividing Armenia between the two empires. The greater part is put under Sasanian suzerainty and is henceforth known as *Persarmenia*.

388: Wahram IV succeeds his father; continued conflicts over Armenia.

Ca . 395: Invasion of Mespotamia (Sasanian *Suristan*) by a nomadic (Alan?) army from the Caucasus, successfully repelled by Wahram IV.

399: Yazdgird I succeeds his brother as the latter is assassinated by his troops. Start of a peaceful period characterised by Yazdgird's title of *Rāmšahr*, "(the one making) the realm peaceful."

400: Possible date of the rise of Kidara to the lordship of the Chionites and establishment of the Kidarite kingdom in Bactria and Gandhara.

402: Arcadius dies, asking Yazdgird to protect the interests of his son and successor Theodosius II by adopting him as his son.

420: Yazdgerd I dies, presumably as a consequence of being kicked by a horse.

420: Wahram V *Gūr*, "Onager Hunter," has to deal with several pretenders upon succeeding his father Yazdgerd I.

ca. 430: Invasion of Bactria by the Hephthalites; Wahram V settles a border with them near Marw. Relatively peaceful reign marked by great prosperity and artistic achievements.

438: Succession of Yazdgerd II; campaigns to stop the Hephthalite advancements in Khurasan.

451: the efforts of Yazdgerd and his minister Mihr-Narseh in converting the Armenian nobility to Zoroastrianism ends in the *Battle of Avarayr* (26 May).

457: Hormizd III succeeds his father.

459: Peroz, the son of Yazdgerd II and the governor of Sistan, usurps the Sasanian crown with the help of the Hephthalite army.

467: the joint campaign of Peroz and the Hephthalites removes the Kidarites from power north of the Hindu-Kush.

469: Start of Peroz' campaigns against the Hephthalites.

484: Peroz is defeated and killed, possibly near Marw, by the Hephthalites under their king Akhshunwar. The Sasanian court has to pay a large sum as reparations.

484-488: Walash, the brother of Peroz, rules the shattered Sasanian Empire.

488: Kavad, the son of Peroz, removes Walash with the help of the Hephthalites.

496: Kavad is removed from the throne by rebellious Sasanian nobles and clergy.

496-498: Zamasp, the brother of Kavad, as the Sasanian puppet king.

498: Kavad is restored to the throne with the help of the Hephthalites.

501: The Roman Emperor Anastasius starts the fortification of the border town of Dara, near Nisibis, giving pretext to Kavad's invasion of Roman Syria.

505: Kavad captures Amida and Theodosiopolis.

506: Peace treaty provides for a regular payment of fees by the Romans to the Sasanians for the upkeep of the fortification in the Caucasus.

Ca. 530: Rise of *Mazdak* and his *Mazdakite* movement, the greatest threat to the established Zoroastrian clerical system.

531: Khosrow I Anusheruwan, "of Immortal Soul," removes his father and succeeds to the throne. Massacre of the Mazdakites.

532: Khosrow I negotiates with Justinian I, guaranteeing the freedom and safety of the scholars who had fled Byzantium following the closure of the Academy of Athens in 529.

540: Start of new campaigns against Roman Syria. Khosrow conquers Amida and Antioch and deports their inhabitants to Mesopotamia and Khuzistan.

562: Peace treaty between Byzantium and the Sasanians.

570: A joint force of the Sasanians and the Western Türks defeats the Hephthalites.

570-78: Sasanian conquest of Yemen and defeat of its Ethiopian overlords; control of the western Indian Ocean trade.

570: The traditional date of the birth of Muhammad, the prophet of Islam.

579: Hormizd IV succeeds his father on the throne; relative

period of peace despite on-going conflicts with Byzantium.

588: Wahram Cobin, a Mihranid general, defeats the Western Türk forces in Khorasan.

590: Hormizd IV is assassinated by his guards.

590: Wahram Cobin, under the pretence of avenging Hormizd IV, removes his son Khosrow from the throne and crowns himself Wahram VI, the first non-Sasanian to do so.

591: Khosrow II Aparviz, with the help of troops provided by the Byzantine Emperor Maurice, recaptures his throne; some early threats by his maternal uncle, Wistahm, a pretender to the throne.

602: Khosrow invades Byzantine Syria upon the murder of Maurice by Phocas.

602-627: Sasanian troops under the command of generals Shahrwaraz and Shahin conquer Syria, Anatolia, and Egypt and put Constantinople under siege.

628: the new Byzantine emperor, Heraclius, with the help of the Alans in northern Caucasus, routes the Sasanians from the northwest. Khosrow II is deposed and murdered by his courtiers.

628: Kavad II Shiroē is installed, but survives only a few months and perishes in the "the Plague of Shiroē." He does manage to kill most of his closest male relatives.

628-629: the young Ardashir III is installed in place of his father Shiroē.

620-630: Bōrān, a daughter of Khosrow II, rules for over a year as Queen.

630: Shahrwaraz, commander of the Sasanian army during the invasion of Syria, usurps the crown.

631: Azarmiduxt, another daughter of Khosrow II, is installed as Queen and is shortly after assassinated. A number of pretenders attempt to mount the throne.

632: Yazdgerd III, a grandson of Khosrow II, becomes the

Sasanian king.

634: the *Battle of the Bridge*, the first Muslim campaign in southern Mesopotamia, results in a Sasanian victory.

636: Sa'ad b. Abi-Waqqas, the Muslim general, invades Mesopotamia and engages the Sasanian troops commanded by Rustam Farrokhzad; the first major Muslim victory at the *Battle of Qadisiyya*.

637: Siege and fall of Ctesiphon to the Muslims; Yazdgerd III and the Sasanian court relocate to Staxr in order to regroup.

642: A grand coalition of Sasanian forces is dealt a decisive blow at the *Battle of Nihavand*, ending the last Sasanian hopes for regaining Ctesiphon and opening the way for Muslim conquest of the Iranian Plateau.

651: Yazdgerd III, on his way to China, is assassinated in Marw at the instigation of its local ruler. *The end of the Sasanian rule*.

# Map & Genealogical Chart

Figure. 15. Sasanian Silver dish from the National Museum of Iran

# Map

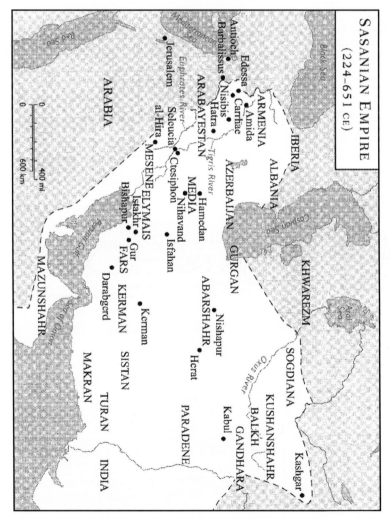

Figure. 16. Sasanian Empire (After Daryaee, 2012)

# The Sasanian Family Tree

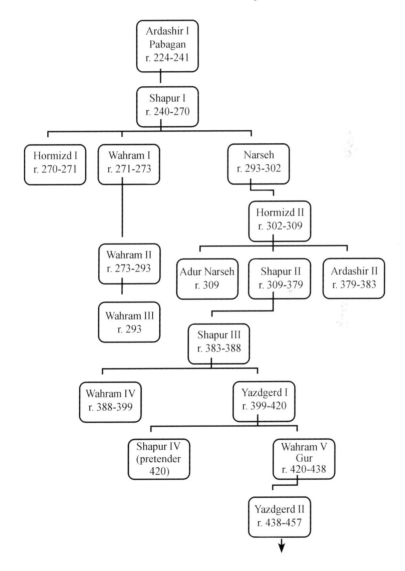

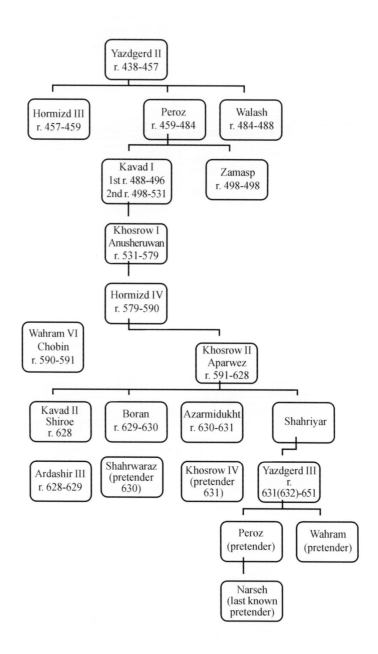

# Bibliography

Adams, Robert McCormick. *Land behind Baghdad: A History of Settlement on the Diyala Plains*. Chicago: University of Chicago Press, 1965.

Agathangelos. *History of the Armenians*, translation by R. W. Thomson, Albany: SUNY Press, 1976.

Al-e Ahmad, Jalal. *Dar Khedmat va Khīyānat-e Roshanfekrān*. Khārazmī Press, 1357.

Alram, Michael, and Rika Gyselen. *Sylloge Nummorum Sasanidarum, 1: Ardashir I-Shapur I*. Vienna: OeAW (2003).

Alram, Michael. "Ardashir's Eastern Campaign and the Numismatic Evidence" in: J. Cribb and G. Herrmann (eds.) *After Alexander. Central Asia before Islam*. Oxford, Oxford University Press, (2007): 227-242.

Altheim, F. & Stiehl, R. *Finanzgeschichte der Späteantike*, Otto GmbH, 1957.

Amouzegar, Jaleh. "Paymān," *The Spirit of Wisdom: Essays in Memory of Ahmad Tafazzoli*, eds. T. Daryaee & M. Omidsalar, Mazda Publishers, 2004, pp. 32-42.

Azarnouche, Samra. *"Husraw i Kavadan ud Redag-e" Khosrow fils de Kavad et un page. Texte pehlevi édité et traduit*, Cahiers de Studia Iranica, 49, 2013.

Bahar, M. T. *Majmal ol-Tavarikh wal-Qesas*. Tehran: Khavar, 1318 (1939).

Bahar, Mohammad-Taqi, ed. 1387. *Tarikh-e Sistan (the History of Sistan, Written between 445-725 AH)*. 2nd. ed. Tehran: Moin.

Bernheimer, Teresa & Silverstein, Adam J. eds. *Late Antiquity: Eastern Perspectives*, Gibb Memorial Trust, 2012.

Beyzanie, Bahram, *Hazar Afsan Kojast*, Roshangaran, 1391.

Bivar, Adrian D.H. *Catalogue of the Western Asiatic Seals in the British Museum, The Sasanian Dynasty*, London, 1969.

Bivar, Adrian D.H.. *The Absolute Chronology of the Kushano -Sasanian Governors in Central Asia,* 1979.

Blockley, R. C. "The Division of Armenia between the Romans and the Persians at the End of the Fourth Century A.D." *Historia: Zeitschrift für Alte Geschichte*, Bd. 36, H. 2 (2nd Qtr., 1987), pp. 222-234.

Blockley, R. C. "Ammianus Marcellinus on the Persian invasion of AD 359," *The Phoenix* (1988): 244-260.

Bosworth, C. E. "The Heritage of Rulership in Early Islamic Iran and the Search for Dynastic Connections with the Past," Vol. 11, No. 1/4, *State and Society in Iran* (1978), pp. 7-34.

Boyce, Mary. "Middle Persian Literature," *Handbuch der Orientalistik* 4, no. 1 (1968): 31-79.

Brock, Sebastian P. *A Brief Outline of Syriac Literature*. Kottayam: St. Ephrem Ecumenical Research Institute, 1997.

Brown, Peter. "The Rise and Function of the Holy Man in Late Antiquity." *Journal of Roman Studies* 61 (1971): 80–101.

Brown, Peter. *The World of Late Antiquity AD 150-750.* Thames and Hudson Ltd, London, 1971.

Brown, Peter. "Recovering Submerged Worlds," *The New York Review of Books*, July 11, 2013.

Brunner, Christopher, J. "The Chronology of the Sasanian Kushanshahs," *American Numismatic Society Notes* (1974):145-65.

Bulliet, Richard W. *Cotton, Climate, and Camels in Early Islamic Iran: A Moment in World History*. New York: Columbia University Press, 2011.

Callieri, Pierfrancesco. "Les Sassanides étaient-ils les héritiers des Achéménides? L'évidence archéologique," in *Un impaziente desiderio di scorrere il mondo. Studi in onore di Antonio Invernizzi per il suo settantesimo compleanno*, Firenze, 2011, pp. 187 - 200

Canepa, Matthew. "Technologies of Memory in Early Sasanian Iran: Achaemenid Sites and Sasanian Identity," *American Journal of Archaeology*, vol. 114, no. 4, 2010, pp. 563-596.

Canepa, Matthew P. *The Two Eyes of the Earth: Art and Ritual of Kingship between Rome and Sasanian Iran*, California University Press, 2010.

Carter, Martha, L. "A Numismatic Reconstruction of Kushano-Sasanian History." Museum Notes 30 (1985): 213–81.

Cereti, Carlo G. "Xiiaona- and Xyôn in Zoroastrian Texts." In *Coins, Art, and Chronology II*, edited by Michael Alram and Deborah E. Klimburg-Salter, 412:59–72. Vienna: Verlag der Österreichischen Akademie der Wissenschaften, 2010.

Christensen, Arthur. *L'Iran sous les Sassanides*, Copenhagen, 1944.

Christensen, Peter. *The Decline of Iranshahr: Irrigation and Environments in the History of the Middle East, 500 bc to ad 1500*. Copenhagen: Museum Tusculanum Press, 1993.

Choksy, Jamsheed K., "Loan and Sales Contracts in Ancient and Early Medieval Iran," *Indo-Iranian Journal* 31, 1988, pp. 198-218.

Clover, Frank M. & Humphreye eds. Steven J. *Tradition and Innovation in Late Antiquity*, Wisconsin Studies in Classics, 1989.

Compareti, Matteo, "Chinese-Iranian Relations xv. The Last Sasanians in China," *Encyclopaedia Iranica*, 2009.

Crone, Patricia. "Kavād's Heresy and Mazdak's Revolt." *Iran* (1991): 21-42.

Dani, Ahmed, H., and B. A. Litvinsky. "The Kushano-Sasanian Kingdom." *History of Civilizations of Central Asia* 3 (1996): 103–18.

Daryaee, Touraj. "National History or Kayanid History: The Nature of Sasanid Zoroastrian Historiography." *Iranian Studies* 28, no. 3–4 (1995): 129–41.

Darayee, Touraj. "Katibe-ye Shapur Sakkanshah dar Takht-e Jamshid," *Farhang*, 37/38 (1380/2001): 107-114.

Darayee, Touraj. "The Judge and Protector of the Needy during the Sasanian Period" *Tafazzolī Memorial Volume*, Tehran (2001): 171-187.

Daryaee, Touraj. *Šahrestānīhā ī Ērānšahr, A Middle Persian Text on Late Antique Geography, Epic and History*, Costa Mesa: Mazda Publishers, 2002.

Daryaee, Touraj. "History, Epic, and Numismatics: On the Title of Yazdgerd I (Rāmšahr)," *Journal of the American Numismatic Society*, vol. 14, 2002(2003), pp. 89-95.

Daryaee, Touraj. "The Persian Gulf Trade in Late Antiquity," *Journal of World History*, vol. 14, no. 1, 2003, pp. 1-16.

Daryaee, Touraj. *Sasanian Iran (224-651 CE): Portrait of a Late Antique Empire*. Costa Mesa: Mazda Publishers, 2008.

Daryaee, Touraj. "The Persian Gulf in Late Antiquity: The Sasanian Era (200-700 C.E.)," *The Persian Gulf in History*, ed. L.G. Potter, Palgrave, New York, 2009, pp. 57-70.

Daryaee, Touraj. *Sasanian Persia: The Rise and Fall of an Empire*. London: IB Tauris, 2009.

Daryaee, Touraj. "Bazaars, Merchants and Trade in Late Antique Iran," *Comparative Studies of South Asia, Africa, and the Middle East*, vol. 28, no. 3, 2010, 401-409.

Daryaee, Touraj, The Oxford Handbook of Iranian History, Oxford, 2012.

Daryaee, Touraj. "Sasanian Kingship, Empire and Glory: Aspects of Iranian Imperium," *Ranj o Ganj. Papers in Honour of Professor Z. Zarshenas*, eds. V. Naddaf, F. Goshtasb, M. Shorki-Foumeshi, Tehran (2014): 11-22.

De Blois, François C. "The Middle-Persian Funerary Inscription from Constantinople: Sasanian or Post-Sasanian?" *Studia*

*Iranica* 19, 1990, pp. 209-218.

De Blois, François. *Burzōy's Voyage to India and the Origin of the Book of Kalīlah wa Dimnah.* London: Royal Asiatic Society, 1990.

Dignas, Beate, and Winter, Engelbert . *Rome and Persia in Late Antiquity.* Cambridge: Cambridge University Press, 2007.

Elishe, *History of Vardan and the Armenian War,* Translated and Commentary by Robert W. Thomson, Cambridge, Mass: Harvard University Press, 1982.

Emmerick, Ronald, Macuch, Maria, Yarshater, Ehsan, *The literature of pre-Islamic Iran,* IB Tauris, 2009.

Emrani, Haleh. "Like Father, Like Daughter: Late Sasanian Imperial Ideology & the Rise of Bōrān to Power." e-*Sasanika* 9 (2009): 1-20.

Fisher, Greg. Between Empires: Arabs, Romans, and Sasanians in Late Antiquity, Oxford University Press, 2011.

Fowden, Garth. *Empire to Commonwealth: Consequences of Monotheism in Late Antiquity.* Princeton University Press Princeton, NJ, 1993.

Errington, Elizabeth and Vesta Sarkhosh Curtis. *From Persepolis to the Punjab: Exploring Ancient Iran, Afghanistan and Pakistan.* London: British Museum Publications Limited, 2007.

Frye, Richard. N . *Sasanian Remains from Qasr-ī Abu Nasr,* Cambridge, 1973.

Frye, Richard. N. *The History of Ancient Iran,* Munich: C.H. Beck, 1983.

Frye, Richard.N. "The Political History of Iran Under the Sasanians," *The Cambridge History of Iran* 3(1), ed. E. Yarshater, Cambridge: CUP (1983): 116-180.

Gariboldi, A. *Il regno di Xusraw dall'anima immortale. Riforme economiche e rivolte sociali nell,* Mimesis, 2006.

Gignoux, Philippe. "L'Inscription de kirdīr a Naqš-I Rustan,"

*Studia Iranica* 1, 1972, pp. 177-203.

Göbl, Robert. *Dokumente zur Geschichte der iranischen Hunnen in Baktrien und Indien*. Wiesbaden: Otto Harrassowitz Verlag, 1967.

Göbl, Robert. *Sasanian Numismatics*, Braunschweig: Klinkhardt & Biermann, 1971.

Grenet, Frantz. "Regional Interaction in Central Asia and Northwest India in the Kidarite and Hephthalite Periods." In Nicholas Sims-Williams (ed.) *Indo-Iranian Languages and Peoples*, 203–24. Proceedings of the British Academy 116. Oxford: Oxford University Press, 2002.

Grenet, Frantz, and E. de la Vaissiere. "The Last Days of Panjikent." *Silk Road Art and Archaeology* 8 (2002).

Gyeslen, Rika. *La Geographie Administrative de L'Empire Sassanide – Les Temoignages Sigillographiques*, *ResOrientales* I, Paris, 1989.

Gyselen, Rika. *The Four Generals of the Sasanian Empire: Some Sigillographic Evidence*. Rome: Istituto italiano per l'Africa e l'Oriente, 2001.

Gyselen, Rika. *Sasanian Seals and Sealings in the A. Saeedi Collection*. Leuven: Peeters, 2007

Gyselen, Rika. "Romans and Sasanians in the Third Century. Propaganda warfare and ambiguous imagery." In H. Börm/J. Wiesehöfer (eds) *Commutatio Et Contentio: Studies in the Late Roman, Sasanian, and Early Islamic Near East: in Memory of Zeev Rubin* Düsseldorf: Wellem (2010): 71-87.

Harmatta, Janos. "Annexation of the Hephthalite vassal king doms by the Western Türks." *History of Humanity* 3, Paris: UNESCO (1996): 475-476.

Harper, Prudence, O. *Silver Vessels of the Sasanian Period*, New York, 1981.

Herrmann, Georgina, and Vesta S. Curtis. "Sasanian Rock Reliefs." *Encyclopaedia Iranica*, 2002.

Herzfeld, Ernst. *Kushano-Sasanian Coins*. Kalkata: Government of India, Central Publication Branch, 1930.

Hodgson, Marshall G. *The Venture of Islam*, vol. I, Chicago: Chicago University Press, 1975.

Honigmann, Ernest and André Maricq. *Recherches sur les "Res gestae divi Saporis"*. Brussels: Palais des académies, 1953.

Howard-Johnston, James. "Heraclius' Persian Campaigns and the Revival of the East Roman Empire, 622-630." *War in History* 6, no. 1 (1999): 1-44.

Howard-Johnston, James. *East Rome, Sasanian Persia and the End of Late Antiquity*, Variorum Collected Studies Series, Aldershot: Ashgate, 2006.

Hua, T. "The Muslim Qarakhanids and Their Invented Ethnic Identity," *Islamisation de l'Asie Centrale: Processus lo caux d'acculturation du VIIe au XIe siècle*, ed. Étienne de la Vaissière, *Studia Iranica* Cahier 39, Paris, 2008, pp. 339-350.

Humbach, Helmut ., and Skjærvø, Prods Oktor. *The Sasanian Inscription of Paikuli*. Wiesbaden: Dr. Ludwig Reichert Verlag, (1978 -1983).

Huyse, Philip, *Die dreisprachige Inschrift Šābuhrs I. an der Ka'ba-i Zardušt (ŠKZ)* 2 Volumes, London, 1999.

Huyse, Philip. "Le revendication de territoires achéménides par les Sassanides: Un réaliteé historique?," in *Cahiers du Studia Iranica*, vol. 25, 2002, 297-311.

Huyse, Philip. "Inscriptional literature in *The Literature of pre-Islamic Iran: A Companion to A History of Persian Literature*, eds. Emmerick, Ronald E. and Macuch, Maria, Lndon, 2009, pp. 72-115.

James Russell, "Kartīr and Mānī: A Shamanistic Model of Their Conflict," in Dina Amin and Manuchehr Kasheff, eds., Iranica Varia: Papers in Honor of Professor Ehsan Yarshater, Acta Iranica 30, Leiden, 1990, pp. 180-93.

Johnson, Scott, F. *The Oxford Handbook of Late Antiquity*, Oxford: Oxford University Press, 2012.

Kaim, Barbara. "Investiture or Mithra: Towards a New Interpretation of So Called Investiture Scenes in Parthian and Sasanian Art," *Iranica Antiqua* (2009) 403-415.

Kettenhofen, Erich. *Tirdad Und Die Inschrift von Paikuli*. Vol. 3. Wiesbaden: Dr. Ludwig Reichert Verlag, 1995.

Klima, Ottakar. "Bahram V," *Encyclopaedia Iranica*, 1988.

Kolesnikov, Aliy I. *Sasanian Iran: History and Culture*, St. Petersburg: Nestor-Historia, 2012.

Kreyenbroek, Philip G., "Zoroastrianism under the Sasanians," in *Teachers and Teachings in the Good Religion: Opera Minora on Zoroastrianism*, ed. Kianoosh Rezania, Otto Harrassowitz, Wiesbaden, 2013, pp. 19-50.

Levit-Tawil, Dalia. "The Sasanian Rock Relief at Darabgird-A Re-Evaluation." *Journal of Near Eastern Studies*, 1992, 161–80.

Litvinsky, Boris A. "The Hephthalite Empire." *History of civilizations of Central Asia* 3, Paris: UNESCO (1996): 135-62.

Lubotsky, Alexander. "Avestan xvarənah-: etymology and concept," *Sprache und Kultur. Akten der X. Fachtagung der Indogermanischen Gesellschaft Innsbruck, 22.-28. September 1996*, edited by W. Meid, Innsbruck, 1998, pp. 479-488.

Lukonin, V. Grigorevich. *Iran v èpokhu pervykh Sasanidov: ocherki po istorii kul'tury*, Leningrad, 1961.

Lukonin, V. Grigorevich. *Kul'tura sasanidskogo Irana. Iran v III-V vv.*, Moscow, 1969

MacKenzie, David, N. "Kerdir's Inscription." *Iranische Denkmäler*, fasc 13 (1989): 35-72.

Mackintosh, Marjorie C. "Roman Influences on the Victory Reliefs of Shapur I of Persia." *California Studies in Classical Antiquity*, 1973, 181–203.

Macuch, Maria. *Rechtskasuistik und Gerichtspraxis zu Beginn des siebenten Jahrhunderts in Iran: die Rechtssamlung des*

*Farrohmard i Wahrāmān*. Wiesbaden: Otto Harrassowitz Verlag, 1993.

Macuch, Maria. "Pahlavi Literature," in *The Literature of Pre-Islamic Iran*, eds. Emmerick, Ronald E. & Macuch, Maria, IB Tauris, 2009, pp. 116-90.

MacCullough, William S., *A Short History of Syriac Christianity to the Rise of Islam*. Chico, CA: Scholars Press, 1982.

McDonough, Scott. "A Question of Faith? Persecution and Political Centralization in the Sasanian Empire of Yazdgard II (438–457 CE)." In *Violence in Late Antiquity. Perceptions and Practices*, edited by H.A. Drake, 2006, 69–81.

McDonough, Scott. "A Second Constantine?: The Sasanian King Yazdgard in Christian History and Historiography." *Journal of Late Antiquity* 1, no. 1 (2008): 127-140.

McDonough, Scott. "Bishops or Bureaucrats? Christian Clergy and the State in the Middle Sasanian Period." In *Current Research in Sasanian Archaeology, Art and History, British Archaeological Reports International Series 1810*, edited by D. Kennet and P. Luft, 2008, 87–92.

McDonough, Scott. "The Legs of the Throne: Kings, Elites and Subjects in Sasanian Iran (c. 220–651 CE)." In *the Roman Empire in Context: Historical and Comparative Perspectives*, edited by J.P. Arnason and K.A. Raaflaub. West Sussex: John Wiley & Sons, 2011.

Millar, Fergus. *The Roman Near East: 31 BC-AD 337*, Harvard University Press, 1995)

Mokhtarian, Jason M., *Rabbis, Sorcerers, Kings, and Priests: The Culture of the Talmud in Ancient Iran*, UC Press, 2015.

Morony, Michael G. *Iraq After Muslim Conquest*, Princeton: Princeton University Press, 1983.

Morony, Michael G. "Land Use and Settlement Patterns in Late Sasanian and Early Islamic Iraq," in G.R.O. King and Averil Cameron, *The Byzantine and Early Islamic Near*

*East, II Land Use and Settlement Patterns,* Princeton: Darwin Press, 1994, 221-229.

Morony, Michael G. "Sāsānids," *Encyclopaedia of Islam,* 2nd Ed., 1998.

Morony, Michael G. "Economic Boundaries? Late Antiquity and Early Islam." *Journal of the Economic and Social History of the Orient* 47, no. 2 (2004): 166–194.

Morony, Michael G. "'For whom does the writer write?' the First Bubonic Plague Pandemic according to Syriac sources." In Lester K. Little (ed.) *Plague and the End of Antiquity,* Cambridge: CUP (2007): 59-86.

Motahari, Morteza. *"Khadamāt-e Moteqābel-e Islām va Irān,"* Tehran: Sadra, 1375.

Neely, James A. "Sassanian and early Islamic water-control and irrigation systems on the Deh Luran plain, Iran." *Irrigation's Impact on Society.* Tucson: University of Arizona Press, 1974: 21-42.

Nikitin, Alexander. "Notes on the Chronology of the Kushano-Sasanian kingdom." *Coins, Art, and Chronology. Essays on the pre-Islamic History of the Indo-Iranian Borderlands,* Vienna: OeAW (1999): 259-263.

Omrani Rekavandi, Hamid and Wilkinson, Tony, Nokandeh, Jabraiel, and Sauer, Eberhard. *Persia's Imperial Power in Late Antiquity: The Great Wall of Gorgan and the Frontier Landscapes of Sasanian Iran,* Oxford: Oxbow Book, 2013.

Panaino, Antonio. "The King and the Gods in the Sasanian Royal Ideology," Sources pour l'histoire et la géographie du monde iranien (224-710), ed. R. Gyselen, Res Orientales XVIII, Bure-sur Yvette, (2009): 209-256.

Paul, Ludwig (ed.) *Persian Origins: Early Judaeo-Persian and the Emergence of New Persian: Collected Papers of the Symposium, Göttingen 1999.* Wiesbaden: Otto Harrassowitz Verlag, 2003.

Payne, Richard E., *A State of Mixture: Christians, Zoroastrians, and Iranian Political Culture in Late Antiquity*, UC Press, 2015.

Payne, Richard E. "The Reinvention of Iran: The Sasanian Empire and the Huns," The Cambridge Companion to the Age of Attila, ed. M. Maas, Cambridge, 2014, pp. 282-299.

Perikhanian, Anahit. *The Book of A Thousand Judgements (A Sasanian Law-Book)*, translated by Nina Garsoian, Costa Mesa: Mazda Publishers, 1997.

Pourshariati, Parvaneh. "Introduction: Further Engaging the Paradigm of Late Antiquity," *Journal of Persianate Studies*, vol. 6, 2013, 1-14.

Qazvini, Mohammad M. A. "Moqadame-ye Qadīm-e Šāhnāmeh," *Bīst Maqāle-ye Qazvin*, vol. II, Tehran: Donyā-ye Ketāb, 1363, pp. 7-90.

Rahman, Aman ur, Grenet, Fratz, and Sims-Williams, Nicholas. "A Hunnish Kushan-shah." *Journal of Inner Asian Art and Archaeology* I/1 (2006): 125-131.

Rapp, Stephen.H. *The Sasanian World through Georgian Eyes: Caucasia and the Iranian Commonwealth in Late Antique Georgian Literature*, Ashgate, 2014.

Rawlinson, George. *The Seventh Great Oriental Monarchy*, Vol. II, New York: Dodd, Mead, and Co., 1876.

Rezakhani, Khodadad, "The Road That Never Was: the Silk Road and Trans-Eurasian Exchange," *Comparative Studies of South Asia, Africa, and Middle East*, 30.2, 2011, pp. 420-433.

Rezakhani, Khodadad & Morony, Michael G. "Markets for Land, Labour and Capital in Late Antique Iraq, AD 200-700," *JESHO*, 2014, 231-261.

Rezakhani, Khodadad. "Mazdakism, Manichaeism, and Zoroastrianism: in Search of Orthodoxy and Heterodoxy in Late Antique Iran," *Special Volume on Late Antique Iranian Religions*, Jason S. Mokhtarian and David Bennett (eds.) *Iranian Studies* 48/1, 2014.

Rezakhani, Khodadad. "From Aramaic to Pahlavi," in *The Parthian and Early Sasanian Empires: Adaptation and Expansion*, eds. Curtis, Vesta Sarkhosh, et. al., Oxford, 2015

Rezakhani, Khodadad. *ReOrienting the Sasanians: East Iran in Late Antiquity*, Edinburgh: Edinburgh University Press, 2016 (Forthcoming).

Riegl, Alois. *Die ägyptischen Textilfunde im K. k. Österreich. Museum*, Vienna: R. v. Waldheim, 1889.

Rose, Jenny. *Zoroastrianism: An Introduction*. London: IB Tauris, 2011.

Rubin, Ze'ev. *Civil-War Propaganda and Historiography* (Brussels: Collection Latomus v.173, 1980).

Rubin, Ze'ev. "The Reforms of Khusro Anushirwan." *The Byzantine and Early Islamic Near East* 3, Princeton: Darwin Press, 1999, pp. 227-97.

Rubin, Ze'ev. "Res Gestae Divi Saporis: Greek and Middle Iranian in a Document of Sasanian Anti-Roman Propaganda." *Bilingualism in Ancient Society. Language Contact and the Written Text*. Oxford: Oxford University Press (2002): 267-97.

Russell, James. "The Advocacy of the Poor: the Maligned Sasanian Order," *Journal of the K.R. Cama Oriental Institute*, vol. 53, 1986, pp. 123-141.

Sarkhosh Curtis, Vesta. "Some Observations on Coins of Peroz and Kavad I." in Michael Alram and Deborah E. Klimburg-Salter (eds.). *Coins, Art, and Archaeology*, Vienna: Verlag der OeAW, 1999, pp. 303-13.

Sarkhosh Curtis, Vesta, Pendelton, Elizabeth, Alram, Michael, Daryaee, Touraj eds. *The Parthian and Early Sasanian Empires: Adaptation and Expansion*, Oxford, 2015.

Schindel, Nikolaus. "Kawād I i. reign" *Encyclopaedia Iranica*, 2013

Schippmann, Klaus. *Grundzüge der Geschichte des sasanidischen Reiches*, Darmstadt: Wissenschaftliche

Buchgesellschaft, 1990.

Schmitt, Rüdiger. *The Old Persian Inscriptions of Naqsh-I Rustam and Persepolis*. Vol. 1. *Corpus Inscriptionum Iranicarum*, London: School of Oriental and African Studies, 2000.

Secunda, Shai. "Talmudic Text and Iranian Context: On the Development of Two Talmudic Narratives." *AJS Review* 33/01, 2009, pp. 46-69.

Secunda, Shai. *The Iranian Talmud: Reading the Bavli in its Sasanian Context*, Philadelphia: University of Pennsylvani a Press, 2013.

Shahbazi, A. Shapur. "On the Xwadā-Nāmag," *Iranica Varia: Papers in Honor of Professor Ehsan Yarshater*, E.J. Brill, 1990, pp. 208-225.

Shahbazi, A. Shapur. "The Horse that Killed Yazdegerd," in S. Edhami (ed.) *Paitimana: Festschrift for Hans Peter Schmidt*, Costa Mesa: Mazda, 2003.

Shahbazi, A. Shapur, "Sasanian Dynasty," *Encyclopaedia Iranica*, 2005.

Shariati, Ali. *Religion vs. Religion*, trans. L. Bakhtiyar, Kazi Publications, 1993.

Shayegan, M. Rahim. "Approaches to the Study of Sasanian History," In *Paitimāna: Essays in Iranian, Indo-European, and Indian Studies in Honor of Hanns-Peter Schmidt*. Edited by S. Adhami. Costa Mesa, California: Mazda Publishers, 2003, 363–384.

Shayegan, M. Rahim. *Arsacids and Sasanians: Political Ideology in Post-Hellenistic and Late Antique Persia*, Cambridge: Cambridge University Press, 2011.

Shayegan, M. R. *Aspects of History and Epic in Ancient Iran: From Gaumāta to Wahnām*. Edited by Gregory Nagy. Hellenic Studies Series 52. Washington, D.C./ Cambridge, Mass.: Center for Hellenic Studies – Harvard University Press, 2012.

Sims-Williams, Nicholas and Cribb, Joe, "A New Bactrian Inscription of Kanishka the Great," *Silk Road Art and Archaeology* 4, 1995-6. pp. 75–142.

Sims-Williams, Nicholas. "The Sasanians in the East. A Bactrian archive from northern Afghanistan," In: Curtis, Vesta Sarkhosh and Stewart, Sarah, (eds.), *The Idea of Iran: the Sasanian Era*. London: I.B.Tauris, 2008: 88-102.

Sims-Williams, Nicholas, "The Bactrian Inscription of Rabatak: A New Reading," *Bulletin of the Asia Institute* 18, 2008, pp. 53-68.

Sinor, Denis. "The establishment and dissolution of the Türk Empire." *The Cambridge History of Early Inner Asia*, Cambridge: Cambridge University Press (1990): 285-316.

Soudavar, Abolala. *The Aura of the Kings: Legitimacy and Divine Sanction in Iranian Kingship*, Costa Mesa: Mazda Publishers, 2003.

Stausberg, Michael. "The Invention of a Canon: The Case of Zoroastrianism." in *Canonization & Decanonization. Papers presented to the International Conference of the Leiden Institute for the Study of Religions (LISOR) held at Leiden 9-10 January 1997*, eds. Arie van der Kooij & Karel van der Toorn, Leiden: Brill, 1998, 257-277.

Strootman, Rolf. *Courts and Elites in the Hellenistic Empires: The Near East After the Achaemenids, c. 330 to 30 BCE*, Edinburgh Studies in Ancient Persia, Edinburgh: Edniburgh University Press, 2014.

Stroumsa, Sarah, and Stroumsa, Gedaliahu Guy. "Aspects of Anti-Manichaean Polemics in Late Antiquity and Under Early Islam." *Harvard Theological Review* 81, no. 01 (1988): 37–58.

Sundermann, Werner. "Mittelpersisch" in *Compendium Linguarum Iranicarum*, ed. Rüdiger Schmitt, Wiesbaden: Reichert, 1989.

Sundermann, Werner. "Origin and Rise of the Chionites/

Xyon/Huns." *History of Humanity: From the Seventh Century BC to the Seventh Century AD* 3, Paris: UNESCO (1996): 473.

Sundermann, Werner. "The Rise of the Hephthalite Empire." *History of Humanity: From the Seventh Century BC to the Seventh Century AD* 3, Paris: UNESCO (1996): 474-477.

Tabari, Muhammad b. Jarir, *The Sāsānids, the Byzantines, the Lakmids, and Yemen, (History of al-Tabari, Vol. V)*, trans. C. E. Bosworth. Albany: State University of New York Press, 1999;

Tabatabai, Seyyed-Javad. *Darāmadī bar Tārīkh-e Andīsheye Sīyāsī dar Iran*, Tehran: Kavir Publisher, 1388.

Tanabe, Katsumi. "Date and Significance of the so-called Investiture of Ardashir II and the images of Shapur II and III at Taq-i Bostan," *Orient* 21, (1985): 102-121.

Traina, Giusto . *428 AD: An Ordinary Year at the End of the Roman Empire*, Princeton, 2009.

Trinkaus, Kathryn Maurer. "Settlement of Highlands and Lowlands in Early Islamic Dāmghān." *Iran* (1985): 129-141.

Tyler-Smith, Susan. "Coinage in the Name of Yazdgerd III (AD 632-651) and the Arab Conquest of Iran." *Numismatic Chronicle* 160 (2000): 135-170.

Vaissière, Étienne de la. *Sogdian Traders: a History*. Leiden: Brill, 2005.

Villagomez, Cynthia. *The Fields, Flocks, and Finances of Monks: Economic Life at Nestorian Monasteries, 500-850*, UCLA, Unpublished dissertation, 1998.

Watt, J. W, and Trombley, Frank R, eds. *The Chronicle of pseudo-Joshua the Stylite*. Liverpool: Liverpool University Press, 2000.

Weber, Dieter. "Remarks on the development of the Pahlavi Script in Sasanian Times." In *Religious Texts in Iranian Languages: Symposium Held in Copenhagen May 2002*, vol. 98, 185-195. Copenhagen: Det Kongelige Danske

Videnskabernes Selskab, 2007.

Wenke, Robert John. "Imperial investments and agricultural developments in Parthian and Sasanian Khuzestan: 150 BC to AD 640." *Mesopotamia* 10 (1975): 31-221.

Whitby, Mary. "The Persian king at war," *The Roman Byzantine Army in the East*, ed. E. Dabrowa, Cracow, 1994, pp. 227-263.

Whitehouse, David, and Andrew Williamson. "Sasanian maritime trade," Iran, 1973, pp. 29-49.

Wisehöfer, Joseph. "Zum Nachleben von Achaimeniden und Alexander in Iran," in *Continuity and Change: Proceedings of the lat Achaemenid History Workship, April 6-8, 1990*, eds. H. Sancisi-Weerdenburg, A. Kuhrt, and M.C. Root, Leidn, 1994, 389-397.

Wisehöfer, Joseph. *Ancient Persia From 550 BC to 650 AD*, London: I.B. Tauris Publishers, 1996.

Wisehöfer, Joseph. "Kawad, Khusro I and the Mazdakites: a New Proposal, *Trésors d'Orient Mélanges offerts à Rika Gyselen*, eds. Ph. Gignoux, Ch. Jullien, F. Jullien, Paris, 2009, pp. 391-409.

Yarshater, Ehsan, *"Were the Sasanians* Heirs to the Achaemenids?," in La Persia Nel Medioevo, Roma, 1971, pp. 517–531.

Zaehner, Robert C. *The Teachings of the Magi*, London: George Allen and Unwin, 1956;

Zaehner, Robert C. *Dawn and Twilight of Zoroastrianism*, London: Weidenfiled and Nicholson, 1961.

Zeimal, Evgeny V. "The Kidarite Kingdom of Central Asia." *History of civilizations of Central Asia* 3, Paris: UNESCO (1996).

Printed in the United States
By Bookmasters